NAVIGATING
THE CLICKETY-CLACK

NAVIGATING THE CLICKETY-CLACK

How to Live a Peace-Filled Life in a Seemingly Toxic World

Featuring:
New York Times Bestselling Authors
Jack Canfield, Bob Proctor, and Christy Whitman

Also Featuring:
Contributing Authors Liz Acar, Marcus Bird, Maria Bradfield, Natalie Cook, Jeffrey Gignac, Karen Kan, Kate Moriah, Kelly Moser, Kim O'Neill, Angi Ponder Reid, Donna Riley, Deborah Robbins, Jani Roberts, Trisha Schmalhofer, Venetta Demos Stathis, Lea Williamson, and Ariel Yarger

BEYOND
B E L I E F
—PUBLISHING—
YOU HOLD THE FUTURE IN YOUR HANDS

Copyright @ 2020 Keith Leon S.

All rights reserved. No part of this book may be reproduced or transmitted in any form or by any means without written permission of the publisher, except in the case of brief quotations embedded in critical articles and reviews.

This material has been written and published solely for educational purposes. The contributing authors and the publisher shall have neither liability nor responsibility to any person or entity with respect to any loss, damage, or injury caused or alleged to be caused directly or indirectly by the information contained in this book.

The author of this book does not dispense medical advice or prescribe the use of any technique as a form of treatment for physical, emotional, or medical problems without the advice of a physician, either directly or indirectly. The intent of the author is only to offer information of a general nature to help the reader in the quest for well-being. In the event the reader uses any of the information in this book for self or others, which is a constitutional right, the author and the publisher assume no responsibility for the actions of the reader.

Statements made in this book have not been evaluated by the Food and Drug Administration. This book and its contents are not intended to diagnose, treat, or cure any infection, injury, or illness, or prevent any disease. Results vary and each person's experience is unique.

Statements made and opinions expressed in this publication are those of the author and do not necessarily reflect the views of the publisher or indicate an endorsement by the publisher.

ISBN: 978-1-945446-99-3

This book is dedicated to our dear friend and spiritual mentor, Fletch Rainey. RIP, dear Fletch. May your teachings about the Clickety-Clack live on and serve humanity for many years to come.

Praise for *Navigating the Clickety-Clack*

"The candid and vulnerable stories in this book will show you a path and journey to a joyful and peaceful life."
—Marci Shimoff, Multiple *New York Times* Bestselling Author, Speaker, and Featured Teacher from the Hit Movie, *The Secret*

"The message of *Navigating the Clickety-Clack* is this: It's not what happens to you but how you react to it that matters. I highly recommend this wonderful, insightful book, which is so needed for these challenging times!"
—Lisa Winston, host of *The Mindset Reset Show*, #1 Bestselling Author, Speaker, and Coach MindsetResetTV.com

"Living a peace-filled life during this time in history is no easy task. *Navigating the Clickety-Clack* gives us many tools from a wide variety of experienced voices."
—Tasha Chen, Vision and Mind Mastery Mentor

"*Navigating the Clickety-Clack* provides easy-to-follow steps, allowing you to learn how to make positive changes in your emotional and spiritual health. This book is a must-read."
—Keith Vitali, Actor, Martial Artist, Writer, Movie Producer

"I am passionate about helping my clients design extraordinary lives in their Third Act. This book holds deep insight to navigating that major life change with clarity, confidence, and courage!"
—Denise Peterson, Intentional Life Change Expert

"I loved *Navigating the Clickety Clack*. What I liked most was the blueprint the authors provided for getting through the myriad of self-talk that keeps all of us from reaching our potential. I didn't even realize I was automatically thinking some of these things. Great book, wonderful info!"

—S.H. Bown, Author, *The House of Roga* trilogy

"If you have finished living a life of anger and frustration, and you're looking for a way to build a life filled with peace and joy, this is the book for you."

—Melody Chadamoyo, Author,
Relationship and Law of Attraction Coach.

"*Navigating the Clickety-Clack* provides concrete steps to make positive changes in your emotional and spiritual health and to build a remarkably happy personal life experience."

—Bethany Sharifi, Writer

"As a functional medicine practitioner helping women with challenging health problems, I've found that it is vital for them to connect with their inner peace on the pathway to healing physical challenges! *Navigating the Clickety-Clack* is an amazing book that everyone should read!"

—Dr. Ailina Ismail, Fatigue Decoder Expert

"As an international wellness expert, I'm always on the lookout for practical, actionable advice to help my clients live and enjoy a healthier life. *Navigating the Clickety-Clack* is a book whose time has come. We could all use more peace and joy in our lives especially now. Highly recommend!"

—DL Walker, MSEd, PT,
Founder of Correcticise™ Your Life and Fixuonline.com

"If you have finished living a life of anger and frustration, and you're looking for a way to build a life filled with peace and joy, this is the book for you."

—Lucas J. Robak, Wellness Leader, Bestselling Author, and Authorpreneur Consultant

"As an Integrative health specialist, I understand the significance of moving through trauma to discover total health. *Navigating the Clickety-Clack* is the perfect companion to the integrative health practices I teach my clients. This is a must-read for anyone seeking to find calm in the chaos."

—Keli Jones, Integrative Health Specialist

"No words can describe how important this book is in today's everchanging chaos and confusion. Highly sensitive and empathic people need ways to stay calm and centered in order to shine their light. *Navigating the Clickety-Clack* is a wisdom-filled book that shows you how."

—Mary Perry, Spiritual Healer and Seraphim Blueprint Teacher

"As a Soulcologist and Soul Purpose Mentor, I've had the privilege of working with beautiful, sensitive entrepreneurial women from around the globe. Being able to be calm in the eye of the storm is essential to tapping into your Soul's intuition. I highly recommend *Navigating the Clickety-Clack* for all the amazing tools it offers in this space!"

—Kimberley Banfield, Founder of Soulcology™

"Navigating ongoing recovery from TBI and neck injury is tough enough. Along with a medically necessary career change, I could only achieve my highest goals with guidance. *Navigating the Clickety-Clack* serves to help me develop a higher aptitude for calm amidst chaos, with ease and speed!"

—Ana Cadena MS, Former Geologist;
Certified Breath Coach; Pilates, Trapeze, and
Gravity Yoga Instructor; Recovery Specialist

"Sometimes living in the unknown is uncomfortable. This book will support you to navigate those times with grace and ease."

—Theresa Coates Ellis, City Councilwoman of
Manassas, Virginia

"This book is right on time. If ever there was a time to have the gift of neutrality, it's now."

—A.J. Ali, Director and Producer of the film,
Walking While Black: L.O.V.E. is The Answer

"This book will change the way you look at others when they are unkind or are in anger."

—Lee Travathan, Celebrity Coach,
Author of *The Rebel Writers* book series, and
The Tender Art of Extraordinary Thinking book series

"This book will open your eyes to new possibilities hidden within challenging times."

—Harrison Klein, Personal Growth Transformationalist

"In a world that seems so chaotic, it's refreshing to be reminded that we have the power to overcome any-and-all life challenges."

—MarBeth Dunn, Intuitive Energy Management Mentor

"*Navigating the Clickety-Clack* is a must-read if you're looking to create peace and calm within your life."

—John Coote, CEO of Wellness Leadership Academy

"*Navigating the Clickety-Clack* shares the gift of alignment wisdom when it is needed most on the planet."
—Bridget Quigg, Founder of *You're a Genius* workshop series

"The truth of who we are and the potential of our mind is often superseded by the world around us. Harnessing the power of the *Clickety-Clack* allows you to finally switch gears and know that everything and anything is possible. This book will uplift and nourish your soul, helping you reach your final destination."
—Kezia Luckett, Positive Psychologist

"A fantastic, uplifting book by teachers who speak the hidden truths of the universe."
—Joan Posivy, Bestselling Author of *The Way Success Works: How to Decide, Believe and Begin to Live Your Best Life*

"This book is a beautiful reminder that we all have the ability to not only overcome adversity, but to thrive beyond it."
—Tamara Hunter, President and Co-Founder of Chemo Buddies 4Life and the 1st Global Next Impactor

"Inspirational, uplifting, and heartwarming stories that help reconnect us all back to our inner strength and innate power."
—Bruce Langford, Host of top-ranked podcast *Mindfulness Mode*

"It's often through challenging times that we learn just how strong we really are and that we can overcome anything."
—Leslie Welch, CDC Certified Divorce Coach®, Career Coach and Life Coach

"This is the kind of book that makes you stop in your tracks and look up from the text as you realize the power of a new perspective on what is. It empowers us to pedal through the Clickety-Clack we all face, every day. Brilliant."

—Bryan Falchuk, CPT BCS, three time TEDx Speaker, and Bestselling Author of *Do a Day*

"Every female leader struggling with overwhelm needs to read this book so that they can become centered in their own wisdom and more effective in their leadership."

—Leanne Sheardown, Change Agent and founder of Happy Heads

"*Navigating the Clickety-Clack* is an excellent book for learning how to transition out of toxicity and into abundance and peace. It helps to learn from people who have lived it, especially during these times!"

—Charlotte Howard, Business Breakthrough Strategist

"As a pain freedom expert teaching people to be their own pain whisperer, I know the value of managing our emotions. *Navigating the Clickety-Clack* is a beautiful book that you should read if you want to be the master of your life."

—Janna Arsenault, Founder of the Pain Freedom Method™

"As a Naturopathic Doctor and Stress Reset Expert, I help stressed and burned-out women with adrenal fatigue improve their mood, balance their hormones, and increase their energy. *Navigating the Clickety Clack* is a goldmine that can help my clients get there faster!"

—Dr. Erin Kinney

"As a Quantum Transformation expert and teacher, I help people struggling with chronic dis-ease and stress. I've witnessed the incredible healing that comes from being still, centered, and peaceful—healing from within. *Navigating the Clickety-Clack* is a great resource and tool that inspires the reader to access that inner space. I highly recommend!"

—Joshua Bloom, #1 Bestselling Author,
Creator of Quantum Energy Transformation™ and
Executive Producer of the film,
The Ultimate Answer is Inside™ and companion book

"Great leadership requires taking action in the midst of *Clickety-Clack* moments. You'll read this book again and again for inspiration, encouragement, and a reminder that you can move through and beyond any challenge."

—Lisa Marie Platske, Leadership Expert and
International Bestselling Author in five countries,
Turn Possibilities into Realities and *Connection:
The New Currency*

"I just love this book*! Navigating the Clickety-Clack* is a must-read for conscious, spiritual people wanting to create a better life for themselves and the world"

—Lorina Joy, Certified Law of Attraction Coach

"This book helps reconnect the reader to their inner strength with a powerful reminder to have faith."

—Bennie Mayberry, Chief Marketing Officer at SmartBeard

"*Navigating the Clickety-Clack* is a book this world has been longing for. How to stay sane in these crazy times is a full-time job made easier with this handy Earthling manual for living a peace-filled existence!"

—Robin Krasny, Creator of *The Light Show*, and
the Breathe With Me Method, singer/songwriter/
multi-instrumentalist of Robin and Eddy and
The Secrets, Massage Therapist, Quantum Healer,
Yoga Teacher for thirty-six years, and
Award-Winning Visionary Poet

"As a Divine Channel and mentor, I help spiritually evolving women connect with their Divine Knowing and guidance. Being able to navigate the stressful, discordant energies of the world is a vital skill for these women. *Navigating the Clickety-Clack* is a must-read for sensitive women who want support in staying centered and peaceful!"

—Nicole Thibodeau, Oracle of Divine Transmissions

Contents

Acknowledgments

It with deep appreciation that I thank all the authors who said YES to participating in this powerful project.

Thanks to Bob Proctor, Jack Canfield, and Christy Whitman for being such great mentors and for always saying yes. Your support over the years has been instrumental in our success as authors and publishers.

Thank you to our incredible team who brought this book forward to completion and to the world one step at a time: Karen Burton, Heather Taylor, Bethany Knowles, Autumn Carlton, MaryDes, Rudy Milanovich, Viki Winterton, Pam Murphy, and Mark Steven Pooler.

Big love and thanks to Misty, Steven, Nevaeh, Sophie, and Timmy. Maura and I are so glad that *Navigating the Clickety-Clack* brought us to you.

Thanks to Si Si, Fred, and Ethel, for showing up for us in the perfect way at the perfect time. And to Goldie, for carrying us up to this point in our lives.

Introduction

Hello. My name is Keith Leon S., owner of Beyond Belief Publishing, and I want to welcome you to our book designed to help you Navigate the Clickety-Clack. As we begin this journey together, you may not yet understand the title, but I am confident you navigate this troubling place from time to time. We all do.

Back in 2005, my wife, Maura, and I met a man named Fletch Rainey at the Agape International Center of Truth in California. We became good friends with Fletch. Eventually he created a group called "The Spiritual Posse" and became one of our spiritual mentors. We would reach out to him when we were freaking out about money, business challenges, fears, or when we were in flux, not knowing what to do next.

One time when we called him with one of our issues, he said, "Relax, you are just in the Clickety-Clack."

We asked, "What is the Clickety-Clack?"

Fletch said, "Remember when you had a ten-speed bicycle, and you changed from one gear to another? There is that moment when the chain is jumping from one gear to the next gear, but it has not clicked in yet. What sound does it make? *Clickety-clack . . . clickety-clack.* You have faith it will catch eventually, so you keep peddling the bike. Your faith pays off because it eventually catches, and when it does, you are off into an even better gear. That is where you are right now—you are in the Clickety-Clack. Have faith and know that things will kick into the next gear soon enough. Trust, and know that all is well."

His reply would stay with us, and to this day when Maura and I are experiencing worry or not knowing what to do next, one of us will look at the other and say, "Clickety-Clack." Other times I have experienced the Clickety-Clack are when others around me are freaking out, coming unglued, being judgmental, hateful, or angry toward me.

In a world filled with so much anger, resentment, judgment, hate, shame, and finger-pointing, how is one supposed to stay peaceful?

Over the years, I have developed tools to remain calm and peaceful in these times. People have asked me how I am able to do this. The answer is multi-layered, and it has taken me years to arrive at this point.

Here are some practices that have helped me over the years:

- Experiential growth workshops
- *The Work* of Byron Katie
- Prayer and mediation
- Teachings from the mystics
- Minding my thoughts and language

In the spring of 2020, the COVID-19 pandemic kept us all in our homes. This was a time of inner reflection for me. I took time to go within and look for answers to the question: *What's next for me?* I had visions of our dear friend Fletch and his teaching us about the Clickety-Clack. I thought: *If ever there were a time to stay calm and peaceful, it's now.*

With so much seemingly toxic information, news, and energy around us, wouldn't now be a great time to gain some tools for neutrality? I thought to myself: *I know people who are living these principles every day. I am friends with people who are able to stay peaceful, even now.* This thought led me to reach out to three dear friends and mentors, Bob Proctor, Jack Canfield, and Christy Whitman. I shared the title and subtitle with them, and they said they would love to participate in this book.

Next, I made a short list of other friends I knew who were walking and talking demonstrations of staying peaceful when others would not be able to do so. I contacted these friends and asked them if they would like to participate. At the end of each call, I asked each friend, "Do you know someone who is living a peace-filled life in a seemingly toxic world?" The people they recommended actually appear in these pages. It was important to me that every person in this book lives this principle.

Each person in this book is living what they will share and teach you!

I suggest taking your time reading this book. Read one story at a time, then stop and meditate on what was shared. Take notes, write in a journal, decide if there is a next step you would like to take, such as researching teachers, programs, or seminars recommended.

I have put together for you the finest group of people to share their Clickety-Clack stories, how they navigated out of the Clickety-Clack, and how they are able to stay peaceful inside, no matter what is happening outside. May you enjoy each and every word. May you be guided to next steps and ultimately discover what is called *the peace that passes all understanding*.

Liz Acar

How has the Clickety-Clack shown up in your life?

Wow, great question. Boy, it has shown up so many times. Probably one of the most recent times is the coronavirus pandemic and the unsettling times that have not only hit me, but the world. That event became much tougher to navigate because my dad became ill and ended up in the hospital on Mother's Day. He passed away fourteen days later.

Not only was I navigating all the changes and unknowns of a global pandemic, I was also dealing with the loss and death of my father during an unprecedented time. I was not able to go into the ICU, so I was not able to see him before he passed away. Traveling became a challenge. I was dealing with grief while social distancing. Friends were uncomfortable spending time together, so I missed out on the comfort of hugging.

I was navigating all the emotions of grief within the extra layer of the virus, and events were happening in a way I had never experienced before. Learning to navigate the coronavirus and its impact was difficult at moments. It became an interesting journey, trying to find and navigate from a space of peace. I definitely was thrown off my balance at times, but I think Dad's passing made it even more stressful. It took me back a couple of years to a time when I had to face the death of my partner and how lost I felt.

When I lost my partner, I had become pretty disconnected. I had forgotten to use some of the tools and the processes that could have helped to navigate that time with more peace and ease. Gratefully, the last couple of years, I have worked on reconnecting within, using the processes I know. I returned to practices that helped me move into a state of peace and calm as the storms of life became rougher.

I was able to draw from those days when I was having a little more trouble finding or connecting with that peace. I was able to fall back on those processes and tools that helped me in the past. Every day was not perfect, but experiencing even a few minutes of peace and a moment of relief on a difficult day can feel so much better. I continue to practice and take one moment at a time, one day at a time, to allow myself to move through whatever is happening.

It has been almost a month since I flew home to deal with Dad's hospitalization and death. Each day, I did my best to take the time I needed to take care of myself and to remember to do things to help me navigate with more peace and ease.

How did you navigate the Clickety-Clack?

When the virus became a bigger deal, there was so much unknown around it. I felt unsettled. There was a lot of fear, confusion, and overwhelm. It was hard not to be pulled into that energy, and I found myself at times being pulled in. At first, I used the power of thought and imagination in ways that were not to my advantage. I allowed myself to sink into the lower vibration of worry and concern, and then, I quickly realized this choice was not helping. I was not feeling good.

I used some of the tools I have always used with myself. I stopped—just stopped—and took a moment to become aware, focus on what was I focusing on, notice what I was noticing, and scan how was I feeling in that moment. If I was not feeling good, I asked myself if there was something I could do, in that moment, that could help me shift my energy. I considered inspired thought and inspired action, asking: *What can I do right here, right now?* I tapped in to that.

Some days, it was a little easier than others. I worked to find that nonjudgmental place regarding whatever I was feeling. Being gentle with myself and being loving and kind with myself became so important. Some days, I did a great job, and I was really at peace—even at joy. Then, there were other days that were a little tougher as it was an unprecedented time for all of us.

I did not want to dig into the story of *why* it was tougher. I did not want figure out what was going on with my feelings; I simply wanted to honor and respect those feelings and allow them to be. Then, I allowed them to pass. Next, I imagined: *How do I want to feel in this moment?*

I used my breath. I moved from my head space into my heart space and connected with these questions:

- *How do I want to feel?*
- *What do I want?*
- *What would help in this moment?*

I did my best to figure out the next inspired step, what I could do to connect with more peace in that moment. Some days, there was actually something I could physically do, even if it was during the safer-at-home time. We were still allowed to go out and exercise. I could ride my bike outside. I could exercise; I could look for the beauty all around me and remind myself to stop, be present, and be grateful.

Other times, I practiced being present, showing up in that moment, and honoring my feelings, allowing them to shift in right and perfect timing. Right then, I told myself to just have faith and trust that all was well in that moment.

Some days still felt unsettling, but connecting with even a moment of peace provided relief. These were the same tools I used to help with the loss of my partner and throughout the process of navigating my dad's illness, his time in the hospital, and his truly unexpected death.

What tools do you recommend for staying peaceful in a seemingly toxic world?

I have learned it is not finding freedom from the storm. Contrast is always going to show up; it is about learning how to find and connect with peace and beauty amid the storm. The more I am able to accomplish that in the moment, the more peace I feel, regardless of what is going on in my life.

I use processes I have taught to thousands of clients over my twenty-five year career. One of them is the simplest, and also one of the most powerful, steps. I call it, *Stop and Take 5*. Stop and take five deep breaths. When you are taking those deep breaths, connect inside, drop out of your head space and into your heart space.

I call the *head space* the part that experiences mind chatter, those limiting beliefs that can get us stuck. The *heart space* is more about divine guidance and intuition.

When you are taking those deep breaths, take at least five; if you need more, keep taking more. Dive into that space and take a moment to imagine a feel-good state, a higher vibrating emotion like gratitude, love, peace, or appreciation. Connect with that feeling as much as possible and breathe into your heart space. Be as present in that moment as possible. Allow that place to shift. Be still, tap in to, and allow yourself to feel those better-feeling emotions.

When I do this practice, I move out of that stressed brain that is physiologically shifting how my brain thinks and perceives in that moment, impacting my ability to be at peace. In a state of stress, worry, anxiety, fear, overwhelm, or other unpleasant emotions, it is difficult to find solutions or peace. Breathing and shifting into my heart space moves me into a state that allows me to connect with a moment of peace.

Sometimes, that peace lasts only for a few minutes, but that relief can be enough to feel a shift. If you can build on it by trying to connect and sustain a longer moment of peace the next time you practice, it can provide amazing relief.

When life was really tough, like with the death of my dad, it was a little harder to connect with peace. Connecting to even short moments of peace throughout each day was still a huge relief. When things are not quite as bad, it is much easier for me to shift and connect into that space so that peace lasts throughout the day. That is one of the tools I use and teach.

Another tool I teach and practice is called the CABI process. Think of stepping into a New York taxi cab. If you are going to step into a cab, you want to have good awareness and a clear intention about where you want to go.

C stands for *Calm* down and *Center*. Support and calm the nervous system by centering. If I notice I am starting to feel more stressed, anxious, overwhelmed, or not at peace, I stop and take a few deep breaths. I often try to use *Stop and Take 5*. I take those breaths and connect back into my heart space as I center.

A stands for *Awareness*. Be aware. Allow yourself to notice how you are feeling and any thoughts, fears, or beliefs that arise. Observe anything that comes up. Do not judge it; just observe it. Allow yourself to become as present as possible in that moment.

B stands for *Be Intentional*. Remember and answer these questions: *How do I want to feel? What do I want?*

I stands for *Inspired Action*, checking in and asking: *What is that next inspired step? What is the inspired step I can take to help shift into a better-feeling place?* Then, take the step. Sometimes, it is a step you can take right now. Other times, you write a note on the calendar for a later time.

In the midst of a really tough day, I might stop, disconnect, and take care of myself. I might need to take a part of a day or a full day for self-care. Whatever the inspired action, there is no wrong answer when we are coming from that inner connection, that inner guidance. I might think about calling someone. I allow for those divine synchronicities to come up. But first, I stop and make that space to connect within.

It is so simple but can be so tough to remember to stop and act when there is a lot going on. We need to remember the power of awareness, of taking those deep breaths, of remembering to check inside. Sometimes, I tell clients *rinse and repeat*—meaning to keep redoing the exercises—as often as you need throughout a day because those processes are so important.

I remind myself my power lies in my small daily choices that create a ripple. That ripple moves me a little toward peace or perhaps toward something unlike peace. I have the opportunity to make a choice—to create how I want each day to unfold. If it is unfolding a little bit differently than I intended, I do my best to shift it or be at peace with each moment.

Try to find peace and beauty in each moment. *Realize all is unfolding, and trust that it is unfolding in a right and perfect way.*

Navigating the unknown sometimes takes courage. We need to lean into uncertainty and give ourselves the gift of time to breathe and center, so we can shift how we are feeling and shift our brain out of fight-or-flight mode. It is certainly harder to use and tap in to those processes and tools that support us when we are in that space of the unknown.

Finally, my photography helps me focus. It is hard when stressed to hold a dual focus. I can't experience peace if I am experiencing anxiety or worry. My photography helps me remember to stop and shift my focus. It allows me to focus on the beauty all around and be caught in that moment, trying to capture its essence. I think that is one reason I love photography so much. It is calming, centering, and peaceful for me because if I am not at peace, I cannot capture a good picture.

About the Author

In 2017, Liz moved to Key West, Florida, for a healing sabbatical from a significant illness. She has recovered and is still living in Key West. Over the past three years, Liz has conducted over 500 training and speaking engagements on mind/body/ spirit wellness. She is also the author and photographer for the international bestseller, *In Joy; A Guide to Designing a Joy-Filled Life*, and the co-author and photographer for the bestseller, *You Are Loved: An Inspired, Meditative, Visual Journey*.

As a Licensed Clinical Social Worker, Multi-Certified International Coach, Inspirational Speaker, Photographer, and Author, Liz's work over the past twenty-five years has focused on supporting others in living a healthier, more peaceful, and joy-filled life. Liz loves combining her passion for photography, coaching, speaking, and writing to help inspire and support others on their journey.

To learn more about Liz and her incredible services or to check out some of her stunning photography, visit: Facebook @Liz Acar, Instagram @liz.acar or LizAcar.com.

Marcus Bird

How has the Clickety-Clack shown up in your life?

I suppose it has shown up a couple of times throughout my life. If we call the Clickety-Clack *the noise*, I do not know how to describe it. For me, I suppose the Clickety-Clack is when things have shown up to change my direction, like tumbling down a pathway and all of a sudden, the pathway changes. There have been three times that has happened.

Once, I was with the Australian Ski Team, and I had a major skiing accident.

The second time, I was a corporate Jedi and could not see a way out of the corporate world—not that I consciously realized I was not meant to be there. Eventually, I realized I was doing the job for everybody else and not for myself. I ended up giving myself chronic fatigue syndrome.

Most recently, the Clickety-Clack showed up in everything that has happened in my current business.

The chronic fatigue syndrome piece is probably the most pertinent. This illness showed up at time when I was a corporate Jedi, working in the corporate world, climbing the corporate ladder. Everything was going positively; work was doing what it needed to do. I was the senior manager of a national company, flying on airplanes every week, and traveling the country to manage a team of people.

I was sitting in my beautiful corner office, overlooking the city. I was sitting back in my chair, and I think I even put my feet up on the table. I was chuffed, very pleased with myself, and I thought: *Wow, look at me! I am doing an amazing job; this is all wonderful and good. I'm on track with everything that I wanted to have happen.*

In that moment, something came over me, and I put my hand on my heart and realized: *There must be more than this.*

Six weeks later, I gave myself chronic fatigue syndrome. After a month or two, I could no longer work, so I gave my notice. I had to give up my job—pretty much my life as it was. All my dreams and goals, everything I had been working toward, were suddenly shattered into a million pieces.

So yes, that event led me on a path of trying to heal and uncover what it all meant, especially after many doctors gave up on me. They said there was nothing wrong; all I needed to do was rest and I would be fine. Of course, I was not.

How did you navigate the Clickety-Clack?

My initial response was to seek help and to try to find a solution. Going to doctors is what I thought I needed. Each doctor took copious amounts of blood and came back to me with the same answer: *There is nothing wrong with you. All you need to do is rest and sleep.*

Three doctors later, I realized the only person who was going to heal me was me. This is when I went on a journey of self-discovery. Up to this point, I did not really understand the deeper world, the deeper consciousness, and what was really happening in my life and in the world. I was focused on conventional medicine, and I knew nothing about natural medicine. I knew nothing about energy. I knew nothing about Spirit or any of those concepts. I had not done a lot of that type of work.

When this appeared, the only choice I had was to go within. I went on a journey of self-discovery, deeply looking within and around me to discover what this meant for me, asking: *What are the gifts within this illness and this time in my life?*

When I had chronic fatigue, I was incredibly sick. My initial reaction was I thought I was dying. Then, I realized that was probably not going to happen, even though it felt like it. I realized I could no longer work. I could no longer speak to my friends or family or watch television or listen to anything that was stimulating at all. Because I could not leave the house or *do* anything, the only choice left for me was to go within.

In that moment, I was no longer the victim, and I started to take my power back from this illness. I asked: *If I cannot do anything physically, what can I do?* I knew there must be something I could do to help myself repair and get well. I started to go deeply within, and some incredible things started to happen.

At this stage I was so sick, I could not physically do anything. The only thing I could do was meditate. So, that is what I did. I meditated for hours and hours and hours every day. I started to deeply connect with who I was, with the Earth, and with the environment around me. I started to hear messages; I started to receive guidance.

Then, I just had to follow the call, follow the messages from the Universe, myself, and whoever was trying to guide me. I started navigating the illness by following the messages, the guidance, I received. I let go of everything except that inner daily connection to myself. So, yes, I went within. I let go of everything and I listened. And I followed that inner guidance. It led me through a very difficult time.

What tools do you recommend for staying peaceful in a seemingly toxic world?

The most important tool for staying peaceful in a sort of toxic world is being able to connect deeply to yourself. I think one the most difficult things in this seemingly toxic world is trying to understand or find the truth, *your truth*—to understand what is real and what is not real.

In a toxic world, we hear all sorts of messages. We are swayed and moved by opinions of others, media, social media, and all sorts of other influences that do not necessarily have our own best interest in mind. The only way to navigate is to understand what is true and real for you.

You must also move beyond the inner toxic world of your own thought patterns, beliefs, and feelings that you might have about what is real and what is not real. The only way to navigate the Clickety-Clack is to go beyond that toxic self. Go beyond the internal dialogue, the internal rhetoric, the internal messages you are saying and hearing. Then, move through that dialogue, move through those truths you are constantly repeating and listening to, move through those old belief patterns and habits, and go beyond them to connect to a much deeper part of you—

to discover your real truth, the reality of what is happening in your world.

By going deeply within, you can then connect to your innate guidance system, your inner GPS, if you will. For me, that means following the energy. Once I connect to that inner place, I then follow what the energy is telling me. It might communicate in words, images, or pictures; however, most of the time, it tells me through feelings. I ask: *Is this the right path? Is this the right thing? What is true? What is real?* The keys are connecting, following the energy, and making sure you are not buying in to your story pattern.

We are very good at telling ourselves stories. So often, the toxic world becomes more toxic when we color it with the stories we continually tell ourselves. We need to move past what I call *the stuff, the story, and the script.*

The *stuff* is what happens in your world and the world around you. The stuff goes on constantly. Stuff happens every single day. The stuff is not the issue; that is not where the toxicity starts. Toxicity starts when we create stories around the stuff.

We start to create these *stories* around what we are saying, hearing, and experiencing. These stories become toxic, and then, they embed as *scripts* within us. We are then run by these scripts, which are mostly unconscious patterns of behavior. These patterns of behavior create more toxic scripts. When we connect within, we can become aware of our unconscious stories, scripts, and patterns of behavior and begin to move through and past the stuff, the story, and the script.

Then and only then can we connect to what is real and true in our lives. We can connect to the truth without it being colored

by our stories, which may or may not be true. Then, we can see
what is really, really going on in our lives. We can make different
and better choices to help us to create the life of our dreams. We
can choose to follow this energy because it is the only thing that
is true and real.

I teach connecting inward through practices like meditation,
mindfulness, and simple observation, and the continual
questioning of oneself.

Ask the question:

Is this true?

*Is what I am saying and the story I am creating out of this situation
true and real?*

Understanding what is truth and reality for you will then become
apparent.

Truth is a subjective personal experience, whereas reality is
what is. We often connect to the truth, which is clouded by
the environment we are in, the people we hang out with, and
the thoughts in our head. Our ultimate reality is not swayed or
colored by those things. When we connect deeply within, we
connect deeply with this ultimate reality.

If we find our truth from that ultimate reality, then life is more
peaceful and situations tend to turn out better. We tend to
experience more success and abundance, and we can manifest
the life we ultimately want.

About the Author

Hi. I'm Marcus, and I'm the wellness futurist and wellness leader driving a mission to move the world to wellness.

I'm a little crazy about empowering people and wellness professionals to be the biggest version of the biggest version of themselves. What this means is that I don't sleep at night because I'm trying to figure out ways to help you help more people by shining your light, the truth of who you are, and what you're here to do. Sounds a bit ambitious, right?

My magic revolves around connecting, following the energy, and trusting my gut. For me, resonance is the key to mastering everything that does or doesn't show up in my life.

I'm here to support, help, and inspire a better outcome, better life, and more success—whatever that is for you. I see the possibility in every human, the possibility to be all you are here to be. I *really* want that for all humans, especially those who cross my path.

The core meditation I used to help me connect deeper, helped me heal, and now helps me create the life of my dreams is called the Pyramid Meditation. I would like to give you a copy of this guided meditation in which I lead you to connect deeper with yourself and the Universe around you.

Find my Pyramid Meditation at:
wellness.Lpages.co/freepyramidmeditation/

Maria Bradfield

How has the Clickety-Clack shown up in your life?

The Clickety-Clack has shown up many times in my life, but I thought for this conversation, I would share my second diagnosis of breast cancer in February of 2004. I was not expecting it at all. I was stunned. I went into shock mode for a while, and when we go into shock mode, our mind asks: *Why me? Why me? How has it shown up? What is going on? How did this happen? I already had my turn, twice! I already had my turn; it's someone else's turn.*

I thought: *It is not mine again.* I said, "Well, what am I going to do? What am I going to do? What are my options?"

I remember the day I received the call, where I was on the freeway, heading to a huge project in San Francisco. I was expecting a phone call since I was working on a big project at USC Medical Center. We were working the evening shift, and as I was driving there, the phone rang and I heard the good doctor's voice. "Hey Maria, it is Dr. Schierman."

I answered the phone. I was rather rude and said, "I will be there in ten minutes. You know how the traffic is on this freeway."

He said, "Is this Mrs. Bradfield?"

I knew that voice right away. I will call him Doctor S. I said "Hey, Doctor S." As I said *hey,* my heart sank. I could tell by the tone of his voice. *Uh-oh, something is up.* I had been in a week before for a surgical biopsy, and it was a defining moment for me. When he did not respond right away, I thought to myself: *Uh-oh, big problem.*

Having been through this process already, I thought: *Okay, no problem.* My immediate go-to response to a problem is to project manage it: *What do we need to do? Take steps?* Boom, boom, boom. *We will have it removed. We will do the radiation treatments, and then we will be done. I have been through this before. Why not?*

Then, he hesitated and said, "Maria, I would really like to see you and your family tomorrow, to review our options."

That is when I knew the situation was a little more serious. That was a big shock. *It has been nine years. I thought I was off scot-free. Not really.*

When we go into shock, we go into stun mode, we stop breathing, and we have an out-of-body experience. It's like when someone we know suddenly and unexpectedly passes away; we go into shock.

Anyway, that is how the Clickety-Clack showed up in my life at that time. My mind played funny tricks on me. I went into the denial, the fear. *Who was going to take care of my family?* I knew in that moment that I had to squelch my emotions because I had a job to do that day. I had a purpose. I needed to go to work and just get through that night. I decided to deal with the rest later. And that is what I did.

I do not remember anything about the night. I remember walking the halls of the hospital. Then, as I was driving home from San Francisco, I asked: *How am I going to tell my family?*

That was the hardest thing to do because I did not have the answers. They needed to process this too. I wanted to tell my husband first, but my daughter was home and she heard something going on. It was a tough experience. No one got much sleep that night.

The unknown zone is not a fun place to live. I tossed and turned, then went to worse-case scenarios. I am the family matriarch; I take care of everyone in the family. So, I wondered: *What will they do without me? How will they handle it?*

The next day I went to the doctor and checked my options. That is how the Clickety-Clack showed up, one of many Clickety-Clack episodes in my life.

How did you navigate the Clickety-Clack?

Well, I wallowed in my pity party for one day, and then I went to the doctor to look at my options. My daughter said he gave the options, and I asked: "What do we do?"

He then said, "It is in multiple margins, and we cannot use the same treatments we used before."

I said, "Okay."

My daughter said, "Hey Mom, you get your boobs cut off or you die."

I said, "All right."

I had a really tough day. I had defined myself as a woman by my sexuality, as I was taught by our culture. I already had cancer once and had a hysterectomy in the course of treatment. If they took my breasts, I would have no female parts left: *What would I be?*

I felt like I was going to be all *gone*. When I figured out what I needed to do, what I needed to have happen, I started journaling. I journaled my adventure, and I called it *My Adventure in Humorous Emails to My Tribe*. That is how I was able to handle the situation—with humor.

I always had a positive attitude, so I asked myself: *Why me?* Then, as I was thinking it through, I answered: *My positive attitude is going to get me through it. I am going to exercise so the surgery goes easier. What good will come out of this?*

Guess what? The good Lord, Mother Earth, and the Universe said: *We chose you because you are a strong woman, because you can handle it more than most people, and you have been a role model for others. You will continue to be a role model for others.*

That was a big *aha!* moment for me because I had to go deep to find it. I handled it the way I normally do—with a positive attitude and humor. I chose humor, supporting others, and being a role model for others. I counseled others who were diagnosed with breast cancer because I also cofounded a nonprofit specifically for survivors. So, I handled it with a lot of humor, a lot of support. I connected with a great group of people.

I became involved in the Avon three-day walks. I joined the Susan G. Komen three-day walks. I journaled my experience. Cheering others on was how I handled it. Cheering them on. Staying connected.

I had a huge *Bye-Bye Booby* party. We celebrated the breasts that had been with me for forty-nine years. I wanted to celebrate all the joy they had given me in my life. So, that is what I did. Sometimes, we wallow in our pity party for a moment, then it's time to put the big girl panties on so we can get over it and find the the action plan. That is how I have always operated in my life.

Any time we have obstacles, we choose how to handle it. Assess the situation. Ask: *What are my options?* Then, put together a plan. That is what I did. Was it easy? No.

I was gifted a beautiful recording. One of my mother-in-law's friends gave me a recording of a healing, and I was connected to a higher Spirit and healing for the first time.

What tools do you recommend for staying peaceful in a seemingly toxic world?

Every night, I listened to the healing tapes this doctor made for me. I listened to and read different books on the subject of healing one's mind and body. I then knew what my options and risks were, given the various medical treatments available. More importantly, I studied how to recover my mental stability.

What tools I do recommend?

Number one: your **attitude**. I am huge believer in having the right attitude. Anytime something happens, you have a choice. You can turn to the negative, or you can turn to the positive. I looked at my situation and asked: *What good can come of this?*

Humor. You cannot believe how much I made fun of myself. Humor is so healing. Read a funny book. Watch a silly comedy movie. Blast the fun stuff. Act like a child. That is why we had a big *Bye-Bye Booby* party. My brother made me a booby cake. We danced. We sang. Then, my girlfriend wrote some new lyrics to an old song. She rewrote "Bye, Bye Birdie" from the movie starring Elvis Presley and Ann Margaret. We had so much fun.

I had to be strong, a role model. That is how I handled things. I became a role model, and I journaled. **Journaling** is such a powerful tool. I wish to this day I had the old emails I wrote to my tribe. I recommend journaling about your experience, writing what you feel after each appointment, each experience. After the process is over, you can go back and read your journal again and learn a lot about yourself. What you learn can help others.

Finally, I asked: *How can I help someone else get through this?* I am going to call it cheering others on. I am a big cheerleader. I was the first female mascot in my high school back in the 1970s.

How can I best support you? What do you need from me? Take my hand, and I will help you.

This is how I handle the Clickety-Clack in my life:

- I show up as a role model for someone else.
- I cheer someone else on.
- I write about it.
- I find humor.
- I keep a positive attitude.

I wrote this saying about forty years ago: *Ninety percent of life is about attitude; the rest is window dressing.* I keep it in front of me because I know I must approach everything in my life with a good attitude, a positive attitude. And then, I keep on growing.

About the Author

Maria is a Business and Transformational Life Coach. She is Certified as a High-Performance Coach, Law of Attraction Life Coach, and a John Maxwell Coach, Speaker, and Trainer.

Maria hosts a weekly podcast, cohosted a weekly Real Estate radio show, was a guest speaker on Real Life Coaching Academy, and served on The Women's Council of Realtors as President and Vice-President in Palm Springs, California.

Maria has over thirty years of business experience; she has built, inspired, led, managed, and trained successful sales teams for Fortune 100 companies.

Maria is a change angel. Through her energy, enthusiasm, passion, and caring heart, she inspires others to lead fulfilling lives and thriving careers and to reach new levels of performance.

A two-time breast cancer survivor, Maria is committed to breast cancer awareness and cofounded a nonprofit in the San

Francisco Bay Area that raises money for breast cancer research, treatment, and educational programs for the local community.

Maria's greatest joy in life is spending time with family and friends.

If you would like a confidential one-on-one free coaching session, please go to CoachingwithMaria.com/clicketyclack to schedule your free consultation.

Jack Canfield

How has the Clickety-Clack shown up in your life?

I think that the most recent example is the COVID-19 pandemic. I was in India when the coronavirus hit. At that time, we had no idea it was going to get as bad as it did. I was at an Ayurvedic clinic. My wife and I were working on longevity exercises and cleansing, to live longer, to clean our bodies, to eat a plant-based diet, and all that. We heard there was a problem. So, we flew—not through Hong Kong—back through Germany. We got back to the United States thinking everything was fine, and then by mid-March, we realized everything was bad.

So here I am. My whole profession is based on live seminars and speeches, traveling, giving keynotes, and seminars. Suddenly, within a month, all that shut down. The governor said we couldn't meet with more than ten people, and there were no hotel programs. I was in the middle of doing a live seminar when they kicked us out of the hotel.

They said, "We are closing this down at one o'clock." Everyone had to go to a couple of local homes, and I had to finish the event online. They were projecting me on computers with people sitting around them, and that is how we finished out the day.

My team and I were thinking: *Uh-oh, now what?*

I received cancellations or postponements for trainings, workshops, and keynotes. We had about $1 million in deposits for events we had scheduled. All of a sudden, we wondered what would happen if we had to return all those deposits. We did not have that much money because we spend our deposits on paying staff, hotel reservations and fees, and food budgets.

I was sitting there thinking: *I am seventy-five years old. I am in the at-risk group.*

I was thinking about how to develop my immune system, how to stay strong, and how to run a business in front of my computer. That was challenging to say the least.

Then, people started calling: *I paid for a live training, and this is virtual.* The good news is we were able to steer through it.

How did you navigate the Clickety-Clack?

We had to pivot quickly and see what we could do to save these enrollments. What could we do that would keep us from going bankrupt? We ended up renegotiating a lot with hotels. We were successful with that.

We had some online courses we had already created, so we started marketing those. They were pre-recorded, click-to-buy programs—no live components. We really focused on marketing those programs. We also developed a number of affiliate marketing relationships with people in India, one of the largest English-speaking countries where I travel to speak live. I have been there five times doing live workshops. Working with those affiliates worked really well.

I did a series of webinars for three big distributors, for their databases. We were selling seventeen units a day of these live trainings, online. That was really good. Then we started to develop virtual keynotes. I did a virtual keynote with Bacardi. It was a $25,000 engagement, and I was supposed to go to Bermuda to speak live. I talked them into doing it online.

The best part of the change was I would have only spoken to about five hundred managers in person. Since it was now an online event, they opened it to the entire company. Seven thousand people saw that keynote, and I promoted my book at the end of it. I am sure that Amazon book sales went up for a couple of days following the event.

Also, I had a book released at the end of March 2020, and I could not do the usual book tour. There were no television appearances—flying to New York, doing *Good Morning America,* the *Today Show, Fox and Friends,* whatever. I did about thirty podcasts and interviews with people promoting the book and promoting the idea: *You are locked down at home. You have more time to read, and you are not doing the commuter thing.* The book sold out in just two days on Amazon.

The problem, which led to more of the Clickety-Clack, was that Amazon said, "Hey, we have a pandemic. We do not think books are the most important thing. We think foods and pharmaceuticals are more important, so we are not even restocking your book now."

We had to send everyone to Barnes and Noble and then work with Amazon to get it back in stock. We ordered another twenty thousand books, and three or four weeks later, it was back in stock on Amazon. That took a lot of back and forth with Amazon.

I understood. I agreed that diapers and other COVID-related items were more important than what we were selling at the time. That didn't make the process any easier.

Since live events were not possible, I was doing more podcasts. After every podcast, I would ask the podcast host, "Do you know someone you can recommend me to?" They had recommendations.

I have done more podcasts in the last few months than I have done in the previous ten years. I became good at it. I am now known in the podcast world by everybody. I was doing free things, at first, just to sell my book with Sotheby's International, which is a real estate company in Washington, D.C. One of our graduates is a realtor. I said, "Okay, I will do it for free, but can I mention my book?" They had about one hundred fifty people on the broadcast, and seventy-five people bought my book.

Then someone in Denver found out about the podcast, and they didn't know Sotheby's had not paid me. So, they offered me $5,000 to do something I would have done for free. Now, we are going around to different real estate organizations asking if they'd like to host a similar podcast.

We received an unexpected gift. We were forced to act on what we thought was going to be a bonus for our train-the-trainer live program. We have an online train-the-trainer program and a live program. The live program is a large investment; it is about $17,000 for a two-week live program: seven days, five months apart, plus a lot of calls and videos in between.

We had to cancel or postpone that first live meeting, and we thought: *Now, we are in trouble.* We ended up postponing until September, and we offered a three-day live bonus session with fifty people from seventeen countries. We pulled it off by breaking people into small groups where they gave presentations with feedback from our team. The event came with a learning curve and a lot of technical challenges, but we pulled it off. We learned how to do events live on Zoom.

We had an event we had rescheduled for September, hoping we'd be able to do it live. The closer we got to the date, the more clear it became that we were not going to be able to do it live because of restrictions in California. Our first thought was: *Oh, God!* We had to go back to all of these people and tell them the first week was going to be held virtually.

Well, five people immediately asked for their money back. We reached out to them and shared how we were going to do the event, and we were able to convince three of them to stay enrolled. What we found out, which is the good news, is a lot people want this training whether it is in a room or online. Also, this new online format allows people to attend who would not have been able to attend otherwise. These people could not have traveled to the United States because they could not get a visa or because they were from Iran, Dubai, or Kuwait.

We were able to now enroll them for a virtual class, which allowed us to reduce the price a bit. As we do courses online, a lot of my friends who are authors and speakers are seeing people sign up from all over the world who would not have signed up because of airfares, time off work, travel, jet lag, and hotel bills. Ultimately, it forced us to do something we probably should have done anyway, but faster. We are starting to see the uptick now in enrollments and income and are back on track.

What tools do you recommend for staying peaceful in a seemingly toxic world?

There are some obvious ones.

First, there is meditation. I meditate every day for a minimum of twenty minutes. Usually, it takes longer because I do not want to come out of that state. Usually I have something scheduled—much like the interview for this book—in the morning that pulls me out of my meditation.

Second, I have done a lot of personal development work over the years, and one process that has been very powerful for me is *The Work* of Byron Katie. She teaches that nothing makes you feel bad except your thoughts about it. Basically, it is resisting reality that brings trouble. For example: I did not resist the pandemic. When it comes to the pandemic, it is what it is. The question is: *What am I going to do about it?*

I teach a formula: E + R = O (Event + Response = Outcome). So, regarding the pandemic, people want their money back, we cannot do live trainings for the time being, and I've got to stay healthy so I can continue to do this work. By not getting upset about it, I was able to believe: *It is the way it is. It is perfect because it is; and therefore, it is asking us to develop something new.*

I fully believe this quote by Napoleon Hill: *Within every adversity is the seed to an equal benefit.* I truly live my life by that. Whatever it is. Knowing that I've seen evidence over and over that this quote is true, I was able to think: *Okay, let's look where the seed of the greater benefit is.* So, we started looking at doing events online instead of how we had always done them. For me, *The Work* of Byron Katie—just four sentences and then what she calls a turn-around—has been beneficial.

Third, because I use affirmations and visualizations for my goals, I teach people and I live by this principle: *Do not focus on the issue or problem—focus on the solution, and the outcome that you want. Then visualize that.* It was Zig Ziglar who said, "Worrying is visual goal setting, choosing your most powerful tool against yourself." We started visualizing very quickly what would work for us, the outcome we wanted, and the minimum numbers in dollars we needed to make every month.

I have always taught people to have multiple sources of income, MSIs. Bob Proctor teaches that, Mark Victor Hansen teaches that, Bob Allen teaches that, I teach that—a lot of us do. I already had book royalties coming in. I already had royalties on other online courses I had helped develop for other people. I knew I had some steady income. But one of the things that I always say is: "You've got to be willing to adapt and look for other things."

Let's say you are in a room with a hundred doors, and you have been going to door number seven for twenty years. And every time you knock on door number seven, they give you one thousand dollars, or food, or whatever. Then, one day you go to door number seven, and it does not open. What most people do is stand there at door number seven banging, crying, and saying "Why are you doing this to me?" They do not go and bang on door number eight, nine, or ten, to see if any other doors will open.

I was concerned we would need to furlough or fire someone from our team. I did not want to do that because most people have been with me for ten to twenty years. I have a staff of twelve, and we pay a million plus in salaries every year to those staff members. I wondered: *What if we could find a way to supplement the staff's income that was not through training? What if we did have to cut everyone's salary by 20 percent? Is there a way people would still be good?*

We actually found a network marketing company, and everyone, including myself, in my company joined. In two and one-half months, I was generating about $6,000 a month net income, and a lot of my staff are doing $2,000 and $3,000 a month net, depending on where they are and how much energy they are putting into it. We were able to spread out to the world because we have a big mailing list, and it is a good product.

Another thing: *Know there is always a solution, and then start.*

When you are afraid, your energy flows to your amygdala, which is where fear lives, and to the hippocampus, which is where memory lives. All energies flow to the back part of our brain, and the blood and the energy are drained from the prefrontal cortex—the rational thinking mind, the creative mind. The prefrontal cortex is where creative ideas are born and spiritual intuition comes through. Knowing this fact, I went to my staff and said, "Look, no fear; we are going to get through this! Let's all visualize together." Visualization and affirmation always kept us positive. That was really a critical thing too.

Next, because I have done a lot of forgiveness work in my life, I don't have anger underneath, waiting to bubble up. In general, I have worked all that out over the years. It leaves me in a state of equanimity. I live in state of gratitude; I perform gratitude exercises every morning at the end of my meditation so I am focusing on what I am grateful for as opposed to what I am missing.

I do an exercise in my seminars where I put up the numbers two, four, eight, ten, twelve, fourteen, sixteen, eighteen, and twenty. Then I say to the group, "What is missing?"

They answer, "All the odd numbers."

I reply, "No, nothing is missing. What is on the board is on the board. It is only in your mind that numbers are missing."

Most people are focusing on what they are missing. *I cannot go to dinner with my friends. I cannot do this. I cannot do that.* So, the question is: *What is here, and how can I use it?* I think that mental construct has kept me sane.

When I was in India in February, I stopped eating meat regularly. I am on a plant-based diet. I do have fish maybe once every two weeks, salmon usually. I do not eat any sugar, and I am not drinking alcohol right now. I used to drink wine or something on Friday or Saturday nights. Putting alcohol aside allows me to have all my faculties present. A number of people interviewed for this book don't drink. Bob Proctor, for example, does not drink. I think it is not a huge thing, but it is important. When some people feel uncomfortable, they drink to numb their discomfort instead of seeking the source of the discomfort. Ultimately, the source of discomfort can be processed and removed if approached with a clear mind and intention.

About the Author

Jack Canfield is Co-Founder of the billion-dollar Chicken Soup for the Soul™ publishing empire. He is a multiple *New York Times* bestselling author of *The Success Principles, The Power of Focus, The Aladdin Factor, Dare to Win, The Key to Living the Law of Attraction, Living the Success Principles, Coaching for Breakthrough Success,* and more. He's been a featured guest on more than 1,000 TV and radio shows. Jack has trained over 2,900 Canfield Success Principles Trainers in 107 countries. He is the founder of the Transformational Leadership Council and was inducted into the National Speakers Association's "Speaker Hall of Fame." In 2015, *Success Magazine* named Jack Canfield one of its "Top 25 Most Influential Leaders" in the personal development field, along with other world-famous names, such as Oprah Winfrey, Wayne Dyer, Deepak Chopra, Steve Harvey, Robert Kiyosaki, Tony Robbins, Sheryl Sandberg, and more.

To find out more, visit: jackcanfield.com.

Natalie Cook

How has the Clickety-Clack shown up in your life?

The Clickety-Clack first showed up in my life when I lost my mom at the age of three. Obviously, I don't have any cognitive memories of that experience or the three years of her illness leading up to losing her. However, the memory of that loss has shown up in my body, in my nervous system, and in the way I respond to all the other times the Clickety-Clack has shown up for me.

As an adult, the key times that come to mind are:

1. I struggled to complete the last year of my physiotherapy degree, due to depression.

2. My stepmother and my dad were diagnosed with serious chronic health conditions.

3. My husband and I moved through the stress of two failed businesses.

4. Becoming a mother, without my mother, while my family was on the other side of the world.

5. My husband became seriously ill, and I followed suit before he even had a chance to recover. With two young boys to look after, this was quite a struggle.

How did you navigate the Clickety-Clack?

As a three-year-old, I can only imagine I did whatever it took to seek and receive the care I needed. I do know we had an incredible amount of support at the time. I probably developed a few coping mechanisms that worked at the time but later became more of a hindrance.

As far as navigating the Clickety-Clack that has shown up in my adult life, I feel I have been driven by a deep determination to move through to the *other side,* and I have a strong sense there is another side, a better side. I don't know where that sense comes from; it's just there. The strength of my conviction waivers at times, but it's always motivating me to keep going.

I've always also had a desire to search for experiences that allowed me to act rather than ones that stopped me from acting. This perspective helps me move through.

I walk that delicate balance between surrender and acceptance on the one hand and hope on the other. In finding the balance, I find the ease.

Reaching out for support and being supported by those around me has been integral to navigating these times in my life and probably my most important resource. My privilege has afforded me the ability to do this with ease, and for that, I am grateful. I have always had all my basic needs met and more, and this made all the rough moments that much easier.

Receiving bodywork, particularly CranioSacral therapy and Somatoemotional release, has been key. I'm in awe of this work. Studying it has meant I've had to do my inner work, which has been an incredible journey, one that has allowed me to show up as a more integrated person in my work and personal life.

I learned to meditate in my early twenties when I was going through depression, and it has been part of my routine since. I practice daily, and it is a habit, like brushing my teeth. Meditation has helped me through a lot. It's always with me, and the only investment is my time. I don't know where I would be without this practice.

I'm still learning, on different levels, to have compassion for myself. It's still a work in progress. Self-compassion has gotten me through at times, but sometimes failing to have it has made things harder.

What tools do you recommend for staying peaceful in a seemingly toxic world?

Create a practice that calms your nervous system and quiets your mind. For me, this is meditation. The things you do daily to support yourself make the biggest difference. You can simply choose to spend five minutes following your breath, being kind to yourself when your mind wanders, and allowing the process to unfold however it happens—without judgement. The key is to be regular, to master the skill, so you can access it easily when you need to.

Reach out for and be open to receiving support. It's there. Yet many of us, especially mothers and caregivers, are so used to giving that we don't stop to let people in so we can receive what they have to give us.

Try bodywork—any modality that works with your mind/body/spirit in an integrated way. It's all about healing from past trauma, limiting beliefs, and stuck emotions without getting all up in your head. In a culture that is incredibly cerebral, letting your body's wisdom lead the way makes for a refreshing change.

Find a way to develop trust in the perfect outcome, whether that is through a spiritual practice or just by *faking it till you make it!* Act as if you did trust in the perfect outcome. What would that feel like?

Surrender. We waste so much energy resisting what is—energy that can be put to much better use. Feel the feelings bubbling up for you, the exhaustion in your body and mind, the grief as it wells up even after twenty, thirty, or forty years. Surrender and give yourself a break from *keeping it all together.*

And finally, show yourself some radical kindness; treat yourself with the same compassion you would a young child. There is a powerful healing that occurs when we operate from a place of compassion for ourselves and others.

About the Author

Natalie has a special interest in working with chronic pain, stress, and anxiety.

As a Cultivating Calm expert, she draws from her twenty years of clinical experience as a Physiotherapist, CranioSacral Therapist, Remedial Pilates Instructor, and MindBody Coach. She helps mothers who struggle with chronic pain, stress, and anxiety tune into their body's wisdom and feel more ease and joy, so they can bring their best selves forward—for themselves and their loved ones.

These practices allow her to do what she is most passionate about, which is awakening people's compassion for themselves so they can begin to heal and thrive.

Natalie lives in Auckland, New Zealand, with her husband, two sons, and their labradoodle, Pink.

To find out more about Natalie, you can follow her Facebook page facebook.com/findcalmandthrive or visit her website at nataliecook.net and find out more about her programs, retreats, and services.

Jeffrey Gignac

How has the Clickety-Clack shown up in your life?

The most significant time it showed up in my life was when I was writing a book years ago. In the process, my wife came up to me and said, "I want a divorce." It took me by surprise; it totally blindsided me. I did not respond well at all. As a matter of fact, I did not *respond* at all; I reacted and overreacted.

I became depressed about her request. Even though I was doing my best at the time to make great decisions, I could not make a good decision after her statement to save my life. I grew depressed, and everything I did was a knee-jerk reaction. I stopped going to work. I tried to get out of work. It is amazing I was not fired.

I was working in the gaming industry. I started finding creative ways to leverage credit—and other terrible things—to pay my mortgage. In the end, I lost my wife, I lost my house, and I lost my car and pets. The only thing I managed to keep was the job I hated.

I went through this whole process depressed and not making any good decisions. I experienced a pivotal moment where I even considered taking my own life. During the worst time, I was driving down Riverside Drive in an old beat-up Volvo.

I contemplated making a hard left, which would have taken me right into the Detroit River. Luckily I did not. I stopped, regained myself, and went home to this really crappy two-bedroom apartment I had rented in the worst area of town.

I sat down with my back toward the front of the couch, I put my head in my hands, and I started to cry. I could not stop crying. The experience was so intense, I felt like my heart was bleeding out, even though it was not. I looked up and said, "God, either help me or take me because I cannot do this. I cannot take this. I do not know what to do."

Because of all the bad decisions I'd made, I had accumulated more debt than I could ever conceivably pay off. I had no support system. My parents had moved away a year before, and two of my best friends moved an eight-hour drive away. I felt alone in life with zero support. My tears began drying up a little bit, but almost every ounce of my energy was spent.

I flipped into this dream-like state, and there, for the first time, I felt that God touched me. The Source touched me. In that dream-like state, I experienced what I can only describe as several prolonged moments of clarity where I could see not only how I got to that place, but the real reasons I was there. The signs had all been there, but I had not seen them.

Instead, I was focused on other things and did not have my eyes open. I had white-knuckled my way through decisions, holding tight and putting my foot on the gas pedal as I drove myself right off the cliff. In those moments, I was given the sight to see the truth, everything that led up to that pivotal moment. All the negativity I had generated in my life attracted the Clickety-Clack and put me in that stage.

Those moments of clarity actually led to one of the first businesses I ever created. They were a driving force, helping me through that time. Those moments also influenced how my business developed. That part of my life taught me so many lessons that are the foundation for how I live my life now, almost twenty years later.

How did you navigate the Clickety-Clack?

The navigation took a little bit of time. The clarity I experienced about how everything transpired, how it happened, gave me an idea. In the past, I had been one of the youngest certified practitioners of Neuro-Linguistic Programming ever—at the age of fifteen. I started learning hypnosis at thirteen. Through years of negativity, almost all that knowledge had left. My brain was really, really weak.

I remembered we can change our state, the way we feel, from moment to moment, not only using our language but using our physical body as well. My martial arts training in the past taught me that. I realized I needed to change my state, but things were so bad I could not think my way out. I could not see any way out, so I decided to use my body to change my state. I simply knew I must change the way I felt.

I needed to reconnect my prefrontal cords. I needed to generate some positive neuro chemicals. So, I used music and extreme breathing techniques—the martial arts breathing techniques people use before breaking bricks and wood. Those were powerful tools for me. For about a week, I would use these every time I would slip into a bad place and my mind was weak, which was almost all the time. I would use my body to give my brain a jump-start, like an electric shock to restart a car. My brain started to come back.

As that started, I had access to a lot of my memories, a lot of my resources. I was regenerating my access to think and make better decisions. I realized I had no idea what to do. I had no money; I had nothing. I could not think of any way out, but I knew I got into trouble by generating negativity in my life and not noticing the signs. I knew if I started generating positive energy, positive flow, the Universe would give me feedback.

I felt stranded on a deserted road where I could not see any road signs. I knew if I generated some positive energy, even in small things, like making my bed and smiling, that would move me down the road. From there, I could receive feedback from the Universe, and I could see signs. I knew if I moved down the road I would start to see the signs. Using the feedback from the signs, I could figure out what I was going to do and where I was going to go. And that is what I did.

I started building positive energetic equity and karma by doing everything I could do day by day—brushing my teeth, putting my pants and socks on—with the best possible level of energy I could create. Then, I started seeing signs. And I thought: *I know what I need to do. I should write goals for myself. I need to start writing my expectations, things to keep me on track and help me move down the road so I can figure out what I really want to do.*

I developed a goal-writing system for myself, which became one of the first programs I ever created. I launched my first business and called that program *Goal Factory*. It was a way to keep me moving down the road. With all the new feedback I was receiving from the Universe and the positive energy I generated, my life changed bit by bit.

It did not take long. In the beginning, it felt a little bit slow, but quickly, within a year, I was vibrating at such high level I completed the course I call *Goal Factory*, my wife came back into my life, and I got the house back. Well, it was a different house. Life was amazing. Pretty soon I knew the direction I wanted to go in, where I was meant to go. It felt like my life purpose and mission came into focus, and I started one of the businesses I continue to run today.

What tools do you recommend for staying peaceful in a seemingly toxic world?

Use something that creates an early warning system for when the Clickety-Clack is coming or when you will be in it. During those moments of clarity, I realized one of the biggest problems was that I did not know I was in the Clickety-Clack. I was resisting, white-knuckling it, holding on tighter and tighter. I was pushing my foot harder on the gas pedal, making things worse.

One of the tools I use that helps keep me on track is a weekly goal-setting tool. What I do is simple. I sit down and write down my tasks and projects for the week. These are the tasks and projects I want to move forward. At the end of the week, I review my goals and ask: *How did I do? Where am I?* I re-evaluate.

This practice is extremely helpful in completing tasks. For example, I put my self-care on there because it is important. I schedule my self-care, which is often using a program. I like to use what I call *life response frequencies,* energetic support services, and meditation. Those are self-care activities I put on the schedule.

We often fail to put ourselves on the schedule. We do these self-care activities when we have time instead of scheduling them. By scheduling them, we put ourselves on the list. This practice is almost a self-hypnosis technique as it creates feedback about how much we value and love ourselves. This feedback has a positive impact on everything. So, part of writing tasks and projects for each week includes self-care and evaluation at the end of the week.

My Clickety-Clack stages are now mild because this practice acts as an early warning system. At the end of the week, if I notice my completion rate falls below 90 percent, I start to review my self-care schedule. I ask: *Where did I fall off?* If I am in the 90 percent to 110 percent range, I sometimes do more so I know I am right on track. But, if I go one week or two weeks where I drop down to 70 percent, I know something is off. If I review and look at where things fell off on my tasks and projects moving forward and see a lot of them that fell off are in relation to my self-care, then I know I am either in the Clickety-Clack, or it is right on my heels.

At that point, I know I need to take my foot off the gas pedal, loosen my grip a little bit, and make sure I do everything I can to avoid reactions and overreactions because this is what I have learned. Decisions we make in the Clickety-Clack are important. Of course, decisions are important all the time. But, bad decisions seem to be amplified many times over in the Clickety-Clack.

Once I know I am there, I make sure my self-care gets back on track. I pay specific attention so I avoid knee-jerk reactions. I pause in my decision making. I take more time to perform self-care activities, like *life response frequencies* and meditations. These quick tools help me make sure I am practicing self-care. With my vibration high as I take care of myself, I respond appropriately to life.

If we focus on responding appropriately to life—the good, the bad, the ugly, and everything in between—we will get through the Clickety-Clack with much more ease and grace than any other way I have ever tried.

About the Author

Jeffrey started his journey at an incredibly young age as one of the youngest people ever to be certified as a practitioner of Neuro-Linguistic Programming (NLP) at the age of fifteen. He studied psychology at the University of Windsor before becoming a clinical hypnotherapist and licensed Master Practitioner of NLP and a World-Renowned expert in brainwave stimulation and entrainment.

Jeffrey is a published Author, Speaker, and Coach, as well as one of today's most prolific content creators in the personal development space.

His love for helping others transcend limitations and live their best lives has made him a fan-favorite in the industry.

For free tools, training, and meditations, download his mobile app for android or IOS by visiting smarterin7minutes.com.

Karen Kan

How has the Clickety-Clack shown up in your life?

As a medical doctor and acupuncturist, I loved helping and treating people—seeing my patients face-to-face. I noticed my mission was shifting and changing, so now I am helping people online through energy and light medicine. This new practice is so different from conventional medicine. When the call came to possibly stop being a doctor and acupuncturist, I felt a lot of resistance.

At the same time, I knew in my heart of hearts this shift absolutely had to happen because I had a bigger mission. I had more people to help than the twenty people coming into my office every other week, but fear was rising up. It was my own fear about what would my family say. They already had a hard time understanding why I left family medicine, which was conventional. In our community, all the Chinese kids were medical doctors or some other professional. Then, I said I wanted to be an acupuncturist, and they were like: *What? Why do you want to do that? Is there money in that?* That was hard enough.

I was thinking: *Okay, how am I going to tell my family and those close to me I am giving up medicine altogether?* I am a little teary-eyed thinking about that time because I had wrapped my whole identity around being a medical doctor. I was a really good one—

at the top of my class and winning awards. I was a professor at UCLA, teaching medical students and residents.

I was completely shifting to my new passion. I was also afraid of what my colleagues would say. Colleagues of mine in the space of holistic healing were already being criticized, made fun of, accused of being wackos, or labeled irresponsible. I experienced a little bit of fear that I might be kicked out of medicine. I was afraid they would strip me of my medical degree, even though I did not really need it anymore.

The worst part was my patients. They were disappointed because I was not going to be there for them anymore in the way I had previously—seeing them face-to-face, holding their hands, giving them a hug when they needed it. It was all going away. I was giving up on the identity of being a medical doctor.

There were all these emotions around that shift. I actually did not want to listen to guidance. Guidance said to move out of that doctor space in May of 2019. I said: *Nah, I think I can wait until November.* I told patients I would remain a year and a half, maybe two. November would have been two years.

Thank goodness I did listen to that guidance. I experienced a little bit of a kick in the butt, which I explain in the next section. But that kick helped me transition and move past all that fear.

How did you navigate the Clickety-Clack?

There is a technique I teach my clients that I use every day. It is sort of like *training wheels for Divine Knowing.* Divine Knowing—also known as *claircognizance*—is knowing the truth from within and being able to take action.

So, I thought: *What the heck! I am going to ask and see what is a good time: What is a good time to transition out of the medical doctor-acupuncturist label in-office sessions to being completely online? What is a good time to close my office with everything I will deal with emotionally, physically, all that kind of stuff?*

I navigated the Clickety-Clack using these steps:

1. First step: I aligned to Source. Some people call it *Zero Point*. I did it by going into Stillness.

2. Second step: I asked the question. In this case I asked: *When would be the best time, the ideal time, for me to transition from my physical office, my brick-and-mortar practice, to my home office, working completely online?*

3. Third step: I allowed the answer to come through my body. In this case, the answer came through the technique called Divine Muscle Testing™.

I did those three things, and interestingly, I received the answer: May of 2019. Immediately, I went into resistance. I thought: *I can't shift that quickly. Five months is too soon!*

Then something happened in my life where the Universe spoke: *Excuse me, but you know what happens when you do not listen to guidance.*

Something odd happened in my practice wherein another doctor reported me to the New York State Office of the Professions, the folks who police doctors, for something I did that he perceived was negligence. It was a minor thing, and I thought: *Really? You're risking my license without even having the courtesy to first give me a call?* In a worst-case scenario, they could pull my license for making this clerical error.

However, the minute it happened, I knew the Universe was telling me: *We gave you guidance, and you are not following it, so we are going to give you a little push.*

Some people call that a gentle kick in the butt. I quickly decided to shift in May. I was not stressed by the report to the State Office because I knew it was simply a sign from the Universe. I had come far in my own physical healing, healing chronic fatigue, fibromyalgia, and all sorts of illnesses through following guidance. I knew this was just a little kick in the butt to remind me to follow. So, I did; I shifted out of that whole office practice into my online business in May, many months earlier than I planned.

Of course, November and December passed, and we then experienced the COVID-19 pandemic. That transition time I had between May and November was spent building my business, and I earned much more money than I did before. It was amazing. Some of my patients continued with me in the online space and some chose not to. I blessed them on their way.

My family was completely happy for me because I went to visit them more often. They liked that bonus before COVID-19. By being able to *align, ask,* and *allow,* the answer came through. I was able to navigate with greater ease and grace—with a tiny kick in the butt. And that is okay.

What tools do you recommend for staying peaceful in a seemingly toxic world?

To be perfectly honest, I am not a good meditator. Despite the scientific benefits of meditation, I, for some reason, do not force myself. I choose to not make myself meditate for twenty, thirty, sixty minutes a day, like so many other teachers recommend. I need something that works for me.

I am a busy professional. I love being busy, and I work a lot. I love every minute of my work, so it is like play for me. I had to figure out a way to gain the benefits of meditation without having to invest so much sitting-still time. In the past, meditation annoyed me more than helped me. I watched some of my healer friends and teachers do meditation every day. I thought to myself: *They are not particularly happier, healthier, wealthier, or more peaceful than me, so I am not convinced.*

I need quite a bit of convincing. I like fast and I like efficiency. I like to have results quickly. One day, I picked up this book by Frank Kinslow, *The Secrets of Instant Healing* (Hay House, 2011). In this book, he brings the reader to a point he calls *Eufeeling*. Through his quick technique, I was able to enter this state of being, where my mind was still, and I wondered if that's all there was because it was so easy.

I read all Frank's books and realized I could enter this state easily and be doing something else. I could *be* and *do* at the same time. This was so exciting that I told my clients about it. One of them said he couldn't do it because he did not understand the instructions. He wondered how he could know if he was doing it *right*.

I was faced with figuring out how to teach this person to achieve this state another way. I discovered there was a different doorway into this stillness, if you will. I realized I could arrive at this state quickly by feeling the motion inside my body. I asked him to rub his hands together.

I asked, "Can you feel some energy traveling?"

He said, "Yes."

I said, "Focus on that."

He then said, "I can feel it."

I asked him how his emotions were. He said he was calm and peaceful.

I said, "Done."

"That's it?" he asked.

I said, "Yeah, that's it."

So, I named this technique, *Stillness Through Observing Internal Movement*. With this technique, you *focus, feel,* and *follow* the flow of energy moving in your body. It is called STOIM, aka Stillness-on-the-Fly™. So, people can *be* while they *do*. If you can feel the energy inside your body with your eyes open, while you are walking, talking, or doing dishes, then you can access zero point, that stillness of your mind, by simply being. You can access all your energy circuits in the present moment in your body.

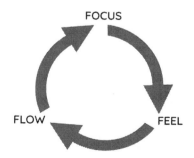

I have found miracles manifesting since committing to *being* multiple times a day, maybe one to three seconds at a time, anytime I think of it. Happy things happen. My students experience this as well. That is my number one tool for staying peaceful because all that is not peaceful dissolves in that place of being.

About the Author

Dr. Karen Kan is a medical doctor, Doctor of Light Medicine, a number one bestselling author, and the founder of the TOLPAKAN™ Healing Method. According to research, approximately 30 percent of the population are *highly sensitive,* and in her experience, they suffer more from depression, anxiety, allergies, autoimmunity, and multiple chemical sensitivities. Her mission is to empower sensitive souls to use their gifts as superpowers—to heal themselves, fulfill their purpose, and create a life of joy. She's passionate about seeing them shine their light so they can pull the world out of darkness.

Through her Academy of Light Medicine, Dr. Karen teaches students her 3-step TOLPAKAN™ Healing Method (TKH), which involves *aligning* with the Source of Divine Wisdom, *asking* quality questions through Divine Muscle Testing™, and *activating* high vibrational healing frequencies. She is like Yoda from Star Wars, training you to be a self-healing Jedi Master.

If you'd like to try Stillness-on-the-Fly™ and the STOIM technique for yourself, just visit stillnessonthefly.com for a complimentary thirty-minute masterclass and downloadable

MP3 guided meditation. You'll be subscribed to Dr. Karen's mailing list where you'll be notified of upcoming free mini-healings, healing masterclasses, podcasts, and telesummit interviews.

Kate Moriah

How has the Clickety-Clack shown up in your life?

There were many times when I wondered if my entire life was just a string of Clickety-Clack moments. It felt like life was always in transition, and it started with a stereotypically unstable childhood. For example, I am thirty-seven years old as I write this, and I have had forty-six addresses in my entire life, a majority of them from my childhood.

There was always this feeling, this reality within my external environment, that nothing was as it seemed. I did not feel secure or confident that I could rely on or connect to the people in my life, the environment, or anything presenting itself to me as stable. Energetically speaking, that set me up for a life of experiences that reinforced feelings of instability and insecurity.

In my childhood, I experienced dysfunctional family dynamics—a mentally, emotionally, and spiritually unhealthy home life. I found myself in typical situations where I felt challenged and blocked, not really checking in with myself. So, I ended up being sent away to a boarding school when I was not quite fifteen years old. I found myself in yet another divisive, compe environment.

Throughout my early life, I felt the world was not safe. This led me to become focused on following the template, following the structure of what I was told would actually create stability and security in my life. I got the education. I landed the corporate job. I had the long resume and the experiences, and I thought I was doing all the things I was supposed to do. I bought the house. I found the relationship I was supposed to be in. I drove the nice car. I made the good money.

I landed at a point in my life where I felt so empty inside, I developed an actual physical illness. My soul asked: *Since you have this all figured out, is this really secure for you? Is it really stable?* My physical body depleted into illness. I actually spent three years wheelchair-bound and bedridden without use of my body. I was completely dependent on what I had created in my life around me, and that dependence forced me out of what I was secured to, pushing me to find stability within myself.

That long journey took its toll mentally, emotionally, physically, and spiritually. I felt so depleted from not having use of my body, not being able to participate in my own life, and feeling angry and resentful about the majority of my life experiences. This point was the deciding factor. I needed to become clear about what safety, security, and stability felt like for me, and I needed to find them within my own inner universe rather than searching outside myself.

This time is when true change and the ability to find peace began for me.

How did you navigate the Clickety-Clack?

As a child, I did not receive from my external environment the awareness or the education to teach me how to find balance, security, and peace within myself. But, I did have the awareness that safety was within my own inner universe, within my own sanctum, within myself, inside myself.

I revisited this truth frequently throughout my life and now have established a practice to anchor myself. When I am navigating any period of uncertainty or instability—feeling insecure within my life—I first establish a sanctuary. I need to feel I can express myself through artwork, through my relationships, or through my home environment; I need a safe and sacred space in my life, so I can fully express myself without judgment and love myself unconditionally.

The relationships and projects I connect to also reflect this to me. Through years of spending time within my inner universe and my inner sanctuary, I have been able to truly evolve, expand, and grow. I have learned different techniques, such as using my body as a pendulum for divination. I have witnessed the miracles that can happen when I separate myself from other people's perspectives.

Sometimes, we are unsure and seeking for that next step, for what feels good and right. We are trained within our society and culture to seek someone who knows better than we do. We seek religion; we talk to the priest who can talk to God because we cannot talk to God. We talk to the doctor because the doctor knows our bodies more than we do.

I was in this pattern of seeking knowledge, wisdom, and understanding outside myself. When I shifted that and started looking inward, I found the *truth expansion*. Through spending time connecting with nature and its cycles—connecting with Mother Gaia, the essence of the Earth—I felt support through the cycles and the rhythms within myself. I started to feel much more comfortable with my own energy.

As I learned to be comfortable within my own energy, I started to feel comfortable within my own skin, my own body. From there, I was able to expand, become much more comfortable within my own identity—how I show up in this world. I recognized that who I am—my soul, my essence—is not the same as my identity. Keeping that understanding at my core is how I am able to connect and stay connected to the essence I understand to be unconditional love.

Moving through life using unconditional love as a handrail guides me through every single challenge, every single obstacle, every single opportunity, and every single event, conversation, situation. Unconditional love is always there. It is steady. It is solid. This love is what allows me to find comfort, safety, stability, and security in all things that are constantly changing, much like nature.

Nature has her cycles and her rhythms, right?

This is the world we live in. The one constant I have found to be the truest experience in my life is that essence: understanding unconditional love and inviting it into my heart space, keeping it alive.

What tools do you recommend for staying peaceful in a seemingly toxic world?

I always love to share. I teach. I preach. I practice.

Nothing is more accurate than your own internal guidance system. That system is your best mate, your best friend, your best support. Establish a connection within your own internal guidance, your own spiritual team, whatever it is you are working with, and whatever it is you believe in. There are some people who work with guides. Some work with their inner selves or with ancestors. Some work with angels.

Whatever you feel connected to or guided to connect with, make sure it resonates with your own energetic signature at the base level of your true essence.

If you experience:

- Difficulty connecting to your own energy
- Lack of clarity about the messages your internal GPS system is sending
- An internal GPS that is always stuck, calculating, or buffering

Here are tools I highly recommend:

1. Exploring the work of Abraham-Hicks
2. Reading Eckhart Tolle, *The Power of Now*
3. Working with a shaman and exploring plant medicine

The first step is clearance. I find the work of Abraham-Hicks helpful in this step. When I was starting out, I found so much value in identifying my own energetic frequency and then becoming accountable for it. I am responsible for my own energy. Once I took accountability and stepped into that idea of sovereignty, of maintaining my own energy and being responsible for my own energetic vibration, the world completely opened up. Potentiality is completely open to you once you achieve that awareness.

The second tool I love to recommend is *The Power of Now,* by Eckhart Tolle (Namaste Publishing, Inc., 1997). When assisting and connecting with clients, I want to bring people back to the *Now* moment because this where we are most powerful. Our past is already gone; our future is not here. We can feel anxious when we are anticipating or planning the future, and we spread our energy thin. If we understand *The Power of the Now* moment, if we understand we are our most capable and our most potent within our personal power in this *Now* moment, we can create miracles. This moment is where we make magic, where we build futures. This moment is where we heal, recover, understand, and expand. This is where the most beautiful and potent and powerful work is done.

Finally, I found another tool in my own healing journey because I had really dense energy, a lot of heavy issues, physical illness, spiritual heartache, and heavy grief. I recommend working with a shaman, shamanic techniques, and plant medicine. It is not right for everyone, but please consider this tool if it resonates with you. I also consider *kambo* to be within this realm, but, as an animal secretion, it is not from a plant. The kambo experience was like a light switch, an intense release, an intense purge, and a complete shift of energy that launched a new start, a new beginning, and the raising of my vibration. I experienced a mass exodus, a mass release of heavy density.

Start exploring as these suggestions resonate with you. Start taking control and power over your own energetic signature, and do not allow the shift within the Clickety-Clack cycle to move you away from yourself. Stay centered and at your core, anchored to your divine line, where your truth and power remain.

About the Author

Kate Moriah is a master Empath, professional Psychic Medium, and Energy-Healing practitioner. Through reading energy and tapping into the Akashic Records using empathic abilities and shamanic practices, Kate detects and addresses obstacles that may be hindering a person's peace of mind and personal expansion.

After meeting with Kate, clients report gaining life-changing insights and positive shifts in their work and relationships, and they experience an overall sense of well-being and an improved quality of life. Kate works with a vast clientele from all over the world and has shared her wisdom on radio, public appearances, and social media. Teaching personal development, energy work, and self-healing techniques, she is a safe and trusted resource for personal healing, growth, and well-being.

Kate's life's work and dedication to the planet is to teach, inspire, encourage, support, and heal others.

Let's stay connected! If you would like to learn more about creating stability within your own life and establishing healing, empowerment, and freedom, please check out the following resources.

Website: BoomingEye.com

Creating Certainty in an Uncertain World Course:

booming-eye-healing-arts.thinkific.com/courses/creating-certainty-in-an-uncertain-world

Connect with me:

YouTube: youtube.com/c/KateMoriahBoomingEyeHealingArts

Instagram: kate_moriah

Facebook: facebook.com/boomingeyehealingarts

Kelly Moser

How has the Clickety-Clack shown up in your life?

Only in retrospect, only when I look back, do I think: *Yeah, that was a transitional period*. I do not think there has ever been a time when I was in the thick of it and thought: *This is one of those transitional moments*. I have not had that level of awareness. I am working toward that, but it's definitely a work in progress.

I believe some or most parts of our lives are always in the Clickety-Clack or transitional time. I come from a small town, Mt. Airy, North Carolina. If you have ever seen *The Andy Griffith Show*, the town of Mayberry is based on my hometown. No, I do not know any of the characters; that show was filmed before my time. But in a small town, we learn the valuable things to help us along our journey.

Number one, I hit the parent lottery; I have the greatest parents on the planet. Yes, I am a little biased. They taught me ethics, to do a good job. In small towns, kids receive the just-figure-it-out mentality, which I believe is true confidence. Confidence is not the ability to do something well; it is the ability to figure out problems. That is my definition of confidence.

In small towns, no one needs to be an expert on whatever the problem may be, they just have to figure it out. That served me in my life. I didn't think: *Well, I do not have that expertise, so I cannot do it.* I have always believed I could figure it out. However, the area I grew up in does communicate societal expectations, what goals should be set.

Where I lived, the goals were:

- Go to school
- Get married
- Have 1.34 kids
- Contribute to a 401(k)
- Buy a house
- Die

Right?

That goal list was given to me as a child. Additionally, another goal was finding a good job and climbing the ladder. So, I got an entry level job with the intent of climbing that corporate ladder, trying to advance as far as I could. Early on in my employment. I said to the boss, "I am coming for your job." My tone was kind of joking with a little bit of seriousness. Two weeks later, I moved into the supervisory role. Two weeks after that, I moved into the managerial role, and three months after that, I was the director of this big manufacturing company. The climb happened really fast.

This is how the Clickety-Clack started. I rose to the top of my ladder quickly. Once I got to the top, I realized: *This is not where I want to be.* I had everything I thought I wanted. I had the job. I made the salary. I was at the top. I had achieved everything. With each rung of that ladder, I thought: *Here comes happiness and fulfillment.*

When I actually got to the top, I was not fulfilled or happy. So, that is what led me into the Clickety-Clack.

How did you navigate the Clickety-Clack?

After climbing my corporate ladder and then realizing that was not where I wanted to be, I started asking questions:

- *What is next?*
- *What is my purpose?*
- *What is?*

I spent ten years in this directory role, bouncing from place to place, always blaming my moves on a team not supporting me, so I would move—a grass-is-greener mentality.

For me, navigating the Clickety-Clack is broken down into three separate parts:

1. The story
2. The search
3. The epiphany

I learned *the story* part from my grandfather. He is ninety-two years old, and I always ask him, "How did you get to be ninety two?"

He would say, "Oh, you know, I just got lucky." He would give some off-the-cuff answer.

He played golf twice a week. So, I asked him, "Papa, are you beating those guys that you are playing golf with?"

He would say. "Lord, yes, but that is not hard."

I was thinking: A *ninety-two year old guy is beating these guys up.* I said, "So, how are you doing that?"

He would say, "Because I play with a bunch of old men."

Now, he is twenty years older than the guys he plays with and that is the key, the story he tells himself. He tells himself a story about playing at a competitive level. In his story, he does not tell himself he is a ninety-two-year-old man and therefore has no business out there on the golf course. Early on, I received this gift from him: *I write my own story. I decide the story I tell myself.*

I have found *the search* involves trying a lot of things. I had been doing one job for so long that it felt comfortable. Moving outside that comfort zone felt awkward. Yes, the search is all about trying new things, but it is also about defining what you are looking for. I don't mean more money because that *want* is surface level. Dig deeper.

What will money bring you?

What emotion will it bring?

These questions help you narrow your search. I knew what I was asking God, the Universe, the cosmos, for this was not going to appear in physical form but as emotion: the happiness, the fulfillment. Lots of different things can fill up that bucket for you.

I like this quote:

> *It is not the search that is most important, rather the belief that there is something to be found.*
>
> ~ Unknown

All the time, we are searching, we are searching, we are searching; and we get so caught up in the search that we lose our belief in the possibility that what we are looking for is out there.

We are caught up in the day-to-day drudgery of it, right?

This search leads to *the epiphany*. My epiphany came when I was at a personal development conference. I was introduced to personal development and learned I could mold myself, learn new skills, and develop beliefs, mindsets, and habits to create and shape my life the way I wanted. I learned to set intentions. Until this point, I was taking life as it came and letting each day fall on top of me. My excuse was: *That's the way I've always been.* Once I had that epiphany moment and learned I could develop myself, life became cool.

What tools do you recommend for staying peaceful in a seemingly toxic world?

I love this question. I have three tools to recommend:

1. Circle of control
2. Power of intention
3. Understanding the truth

The first tool was a game changer for me. My life changed the day I was introduced to *the circle of control*. My version is different from Stephen Covey's (*7 Habits of Highly Effective People*, 1989); it is a little more in-depth. First, I ask people what they complain about.

I was the road rage guy. I yelled at the cars going northbound as I was driving southbound. Yes, I was that guy. Usually what comes up on people's list of complaints are weather, government, paying taxes, traffic, and that sort of thing. I ask them to write that list on paper.

What do you complain about? Write a list on paper.

Then, draw a circle on the page. In the middle of the circle, list what you can control: your feelings, your thoughts, your actions. You have 100 percent control of these, nothing else. Next, draw a circle around your first circle. This next ring is your circle of influence. *Hey little Johnny, can you please eat your broccoli? Sue, can you send me the report?* You can influence people to do things, but you cannot control them. Everything in this outer ring is outside your circle of control.

When I look at my list—traffic, weather, government, paying taxes—these all fall outside my control.

I was pouring all this time, stress, and energy into things I have zero control over. I started to shift, like a light bulb was going off in my head.

The next tool is *the power of intention*—setting intentions, being intentional with how you show up in the day, and not letting each day fall on top of you. This tool has served me well. I use a door knob trigger. Every time I walk up to a door, whether it is a conference room door, a grocery store door, or the door to the front of my house, I always take a split second to visualize who I need to be on the other side of that door. *Who is the best Kelly? How does Kelly need to show up?*

This was a great tool when I was the youngest manager in a conference room full of people. I would ask: *How do I need to show up? Who needs me on my A-game?* Setting those intentions is powerful and useful in all areas, whether it is business, relationships, or any interaction with people. Being able to set intentions moves you in the right direction.

The last tool is *understanding the truth*. I studied personal development neuroscience and figured out the brain is a liar. Yes, your brain is designed to lie to you. If you are walking your dog down a path and the leaves rustle behind you, your first thought is not: *Someone is bringing me ice cream.* Your first thought is: *Crap, something is going to bite me.* That is what your brain tells you. Then, you turn around and see a little squirrel, and think: *Thank goodness!*

Come on brain! We are at the top of the food chain now; we can evolve past thinking we are going to be eaten by the saber-toothed tiger. So, this carries over into our business, where we think: *If I send this very direct email to Sue because I need this report, she is going to be angry, the sky is going to fall, I am going to lose my job, and I will wind up eating out of the trash can and living under a bridge.*

I know the brain is wired to keep us safe, but yours is lying to you. So, when you find that big dream to chase, your brain might say: *They are going to laugh at you. You are not good enough. You are a failure.* Understand the truth, and ask: *Is this true?*

That is such a powerful question.

About the Author

As a Certified High Performance Coach™ Kelly has had the opportunity to coach top Realtors, Entrepreneurs, and Executives, with each client experiencing higher levels of success, increased energy and stamina, and the enjoyment of winning back hours in their week to spend on the things they love.

Kelly's practical motivation and positive attitude are infectious. He often says things like "Anywhere can be your Happy Place with the right perspective." His signature tagline is "Move your BUT!" He relentlessly encourages those around him to let go of excuses, limiting beliefs, and negative self-talk so they can live a life of fulfilment.

As the Founder and CEO of The Moser Movement, Kelly offers Certified High Performance Coaching, High Performance Coaching for Realtors, Group Coaching, and Keynote Speaking, providing solutions for individuals and teams.

His passion and mission are helping high performers reach a new, higher level, bigger than they ever thought possible. This next level is achieved through a scientifically based curriculum that is forward oriented and challenge based, designed to get results.

However, before you can achieve that big goal you must first "Move your BUT!" If you are a high performer looking to take life to the next level, check out my website at kellymoser.com. For all of my real estate agent friends, I have a special program designed to help you finally break the six-figure income barrier while winning back ten-plus hours per week.

Connect with me on Facebook and Instagram @kelly_moser_, and if you mention this book, you'll receive a free one-on-one breakthrough session.

Kim O'Neill

How has the Clickety-Clack shown up in your life?

The Clickety-Clack has shown up many times in my life. One story that stands out happened back in 2012, when I was working at a police department. I had been there a few years, settled in, and I was enjoying my role, my co-workers, and my boss. I decided it was time to begin the next iteration of my career path and move in the direction of my dreams.

I chose to pursue a master's degree. I started full-time in a master's program in mental health counseling, and I was excited to be on this journey. It was a big deal for me to make that decision and take the steps to put the choice into action. So, there I was: working full-time and taking a full-time course load for my master's degree. It was summer of 2012, and they announced at work they were making several budget cuts. They were going to cut the office where I worked.

I was administrative support in the police department's Psychology Office. We were there as a service to the employees of the police department. We'd had a little bit of a heads-up that this was going to happen, but I was certain it wouldn't happen to our office. It did. They told us we had about five to six months; the cuts were happening in July and would finalize by the end of the year. By that time, I would need to find another job.

I felt uncertainty, fear, and anxiety creeping to the surface. I did not have the luxury of time to wallow in those feelings because I knew from previous experience it would take me an average of six months to find a new job. That was all the time I had. I thought: *What am I going to do now?*

Of course, I was already committed to my job, and I was already committed to my master's program. I decided I was going to make it work. So, when I wasn't at work or in class, I was searching for another job. It was heavy. It was stressful. There were times when I didn't know if I could keep up with the master's program.

I had moments of breaking down, freaking out, and stressing, but I was committed to not having a gap in employment. I was the sole person supporting myself. I did not want to deal with not having a job. So, I thought: *I will have a job.* I was adamant. That was my commitment to myself and to the process, and that is where my mindset was throughout this time.

How did you navigate the Clickety-Clack?

My commitment to myself kept me focused. I did not have the luxury of time to be indecisive or to stay stuck in fear. I leaped into action, constantly looking for a job, applying for jobs, and putting myself out there. I was determined I would not have a gap in employment. That focus and action kept me on course, and it was amazing what actually panned out.

While I was applying for jobs, I was telling people I was in a situation because my job was being cut—trying to spread the word where I could. Toward the end of that fall, there was one position within the police department that was not being cut;

the job was opening, and I was actually a fit. I applied for the position, and it turned out I was the top candidate for it. I did not know that at the time.

At the same time, I was continually looking for jobs within and outside the city. I found another position at the fire department that was not only a fit, but a promotion as well. I was a little scared about that, but I did not have time to stay scared. I knew I needed to go for it, so I took a chance. I didn't know anybody at the fire department. I applied for the position. They held two interviews, and within two days, I found out I got the position that was a lateral move at the police department, which I accepted. Two days later, I found out I got the *promotion* position at the fire department as well.

Here I was, blessed with two positions, and I felt so grateful. It was like a dream come true. I was faced with deciding which opportunity to choose: *Do I stay with the job that is a lateral move in the same department? Or, do I go ahead with the one that is offering me more money, in a new environment, and is essentially a promotion?* I decided to take that leap and accept the new position at the fire department.

I could not believe all the blessings that came to me as a result of saying yes to the job at the fire department. I ended up making more money, but I also felt immensely supported at this new job in a way I had never felt before. I absolutely love and support the police department, but at this time and place in my life, I was led to a new place that helped me feel supported, like I had family around me.

I healed aspects of my past in ways I never would have imagined could be healed in a work environment. My career, passion, and skills grew. I decided to move away from that master's program to coaching. I was only at the fire department for a short time, but it was a healing period in my life that came out of a situation that could have been fearful and anxiety-ridden. I am so grateful for that time at the fire department.

What tools do you recommend for staying peaceful in a seemingly toxic world?

There are so many tools. What stands out for me, especially with this story, is how making a decision at the forefront of a situation impacts what you experience. I did not know it at the time, but I am able to now see how powerful it was for me to declare that I was not going to have a gap in employment.

Not only was I offered two amazing jobs within two days of each other, but they happened at the end of my time at the police department. I had decided from the beginning I would not have a gap in employment. My last day working at the police department was on a Friday, and my first day at the fire department was the next Monday. That was the timing.

No one else said: *Kim, we'll work with you. We will try to make this happen.* It just fell into place. I know with total faith that my decision to say *This is what I want* was powerful. This decision kept me on course, focusing and acting to find a new job. I did not receive a miracle answer: *Here is what you need to do.* I simply knew to look for a job online. I just kept doing that.

I had trust and faith, so I did not carry extra burdens I did not need to carry. I did not know this truth at the moment. I had powerful action, powerful focusing, and direction. I know now it is healthier to have immense faith and take care of yourself in the process. Self-care is not to be overlooked.

You are going to experience the Clickety-Clack as you go through life. You can be healthy as you go through the Clickety-Clack. You deserve to care for yourself while you are in those moments of uncertainty, feeling a little fearful and not being able to see what is coming next. Step into that space of trust as much as you can, knowing you are not alone, knowing that the Universe supports you. It helps lighten the load.

When you get to the other side, you will be able to see what has unfolded for you and the tangible facts of your situation. You will relax and know: *I'm on the other side. I do not need to worry.* You will realize you went through an amazing internal growth process. This internal growth experience will enhance your life experience going forward, making the Clickety-Clack so much easier and lighter and brighter. Once you arrive at the other side, you learn that situations do not always look the way you think they do at the beginning. You can use that faith the next time around as it really helps make a difference and enhance your life experience.

About the Author

Kim O'Neill is known for being the inspirational host of the *Every Day is a New Day Show*, a two-times Bestselling Author, twice-certified Transformational Confidence Coach, Interview Coach, Reiki Master, and former Crime Analyst. Her podcast and live show have featured movers and shakers from the White House and national TV to awesome everyday people who've exhibited inspiring strength in overcoming their own adversities.

Kim takes a holistic approach in coaching empathic, intelligent individuals out of self-doubt and disempowerment and into courageous confidence. She also mentors job-seekers and prospective podcast guests in preparing for interviews. Her previous co-authored books include the number one bestseller *You Are Loved—An Inspired, Meditative Visual Journey* (2019) and the bestseller *Positive-Minded People* (2017). Kim is most often asked how she went from being a Crime Analyst to coaching and energy work, and her answer is that she loves to empower people to be who they truly are.

Connect with Kim and download her free guided meditation "Get Grounded & Regain Inner Peace" on KimONeillCoaching. com.

Bob Proctor

How has the Clickety-Clack shown up in your life?

The Clickety-Clack shows up often. I think it's just part of life because you never know how everything is going to work out. If you know all the pieces ahead of time, you're probably going sideways, and the event is a repeat performance.

Whenever you're going after a goal—in my mind—you have no idea how you are going to do it. You only know you're going to do it. In 1953, Edmund Hillary didn't know how to get to the top of Mount Everest until after he reached the top. The Wright brothers didn't know how to steer a plane in the air until they did it. Edison didn't know how to create the filament of a light bulb until he created it. So, when you're going after a goal, you should be going after something you don't know how to do—yet.

The purpose of a goal is to help you grow. You are going after something you want. The *want* goes with the essence of who you are, which is perfection within. That perfection within is seeking expression, which is why we want things greater than the norm. If you run, you want to run faster. If you jump, you want to jump higher. If you are selling, you want to sell more. Whatever you are doing, you want to do it bigger and better.

The Clickety-Clack is when things haven't really clicked into gear, and they're not falling into place the way you would like. I think you've got to persist, stay at it, and know that if you keep at it, things will ultimately fall into place. Out of all confusion comes order—a higher degree of order than that which existed prior to the confusion. It's important to keep moving forward, no matter what's going on.

How did you navigate the Clickety-Clack?

By shifting perception. By looking for a better way, or another way.

Perception is one of our better faculties. It is important to understand things are not always as they appear. Because of your perception, you have the innate ability to change the way things appear. You can look at them from a different perspective.

If you are running into a problem or you've got challenges, write them out on a piece of paper. I do this. Then, I put the paper in the center of the table and ask myself: *Is that problem on me, or is it on the paper?* Because I have written it on the paper—moved it out of me and onto the paper—I can look at it objectively, like a stranger would see it. After I do that, I sit at another place at the table and say: *How would Earl Nightingale look at that problem?* Then, I move to another seat at the table and say: *How would Napoleon Hill perceive that? How would Albert Einstein look at that?*

Because we are multidimensional and have marvelous minds, we can look at things from all different points of view. If we do this, we will soon start to see the problem as a different situation all together. This is why we have perception.

Wayne Dyer said, "If you change the way you look at things, the things you look at change." So, what we are calling the Clickety-Clack is a lack of understanding about the truth of what is really going on. Don't let the Clickety-Clack thoughts control you; you need to control them. If you let those thoughts control you, you are going to lose every time.

What tools do you recommend for staying peaceful in a seemingly toxic world?

First, know exactly how your mind functions. For example, let's say you are watching a movie, and it's a horror film. It's going to scare the hell out of you. Why? Because your mind accepts it as real. You may find yourself screaming out loud. Your subconscious mind accepts everything you give it as real. It cannot differentiate between something real and something imagined. Rather than use this fact against yourself, you should use it in your favor. Understand that if you're not thinking *this isn't real* while you're watching—you're really into the horror of that film—the information you are receiving is going right into your subconscious mind.

Today, as you look at social media or listen to the news on television and the radio, you're being inundated with terrible news. Know what you are hearing and seeing is going right into your subconscious mind, and it's affecting the vibration you are in. It affects your attitude. It starts to control you because your subconscious mind accepts anything you give it.

I am cautious anytime I see a news report. I don't want to listen to it. I figure if anything is important enough that I should know, I will hear about it in conversation as I go through my day. I don't let the news control me. I don't care if it's fake news or real news; I'm not interested.

Now, does that mean that there's no pandemic, no big problems right now?

No, it doesn't mean that at all. It just means that I am not going to allow it to control how I think. I am not going to look at the negative side of anything.

The truth is everything *just is*. There is neither good nor bad. There is a law called *The Law of Polarity*, and that law decrees everything is dual—meaning: Things that appear to be opposites are, in fact, two parts of the same thing. We choose. We can look at whichever side we want to see. We can see the same thing as either bad or good.

I was recently being interviewed and the interviewer asked me, "What would you tell someone who is listening who has just lost their job? They have no more income."

I replied, "Well, they cannot control what is going on, but they can control their perception of what's going on. They could say to themselves, 'I have lost my job, and now is a darn good time to start over. I have the ability here to recreate my life. I probably would have preferred to stay in my job, but it is gone. Let the dead bury the dead. I need to let it go and take control of my life. I am going to do something really interesting with this next phase of my life. I am a creative being, and I can create a new situation. I'm going to make the world better for me and my family with this opportunity.'"

If you leave your mind open to what's going on outside, you're going to be in bad shape. I think that's the problem with 97 percent of the population. They never stop to ask themselves: *Is this real? Do I have to let this control me?*

Is it real? It's not something somebody made up, so sure, there are real problems in the world. It's vital, however, that you control the way you think about the situation and not let it control you.

My good friend, Reverend Michael Beckwith of the Agape International Spiritual Center, uses a three-step approach when anything happens:

> *Step 1*. It is what it is. Accept it. You cannot change it. It will either control you—or—you will control it.
>
> *Step 2*. Harvest the good. The more you look for, the more you will find.
>
> *Step 3*. Forgive all the rest. *Forgiving* means letting go completely.

This approach is the best way to look at everything that happens in our lives. Most people don't know they can control the way they perceive life. People are raised to live by their senses. They go by what they see, hear, smell, taste, or touch. That's limited thinking.

I have a couple of little dogs that can see, hear, smell, taste, or touch, but they don't have higher faculties. We, as people, have perception, will, reasoning, imagination, memory, and intuition. These faculties make us who we are. They give us our God-like resonance.

You see, we are created in God's image. Most people have that reversed, and they create God in their image. They create a real problem for themselves they never figure out. When they do straighten it out, they will say, "I'm in charge of me, and I am going to learn to use all these higher faculties."

We humans are the only creatures on this planet who are disoriented in our environment. All the other little creatures are at home in their environment. They blend in. They operate by instinct. We had instinct removed, and all the higher faculties put in its place. We can create our own environment. Other creatures blend into their environment; we create our own. There is a big difference between what they do and what we are able to do.

About the Author

Bob Proctor is a New York Times Bestselling Author, World-Renowned Speaker, and featured Teacher from the hit movie, *The Secret*. For more than forty years, Bob has focused his entire agenda around helping people create lush lives of prosperity, rewarding relationships, and spiritual awareness. As one of the world's most highly regarded speakers on prosperity, he is internationally known for his inspirational and motivational style. He is widely considered one of the greatest speakers in the world on the topic of getting rich. He teaches people how to understand their hidden abilities to do more, be more, and have more in every area of life. His teachings are based on Napoleon Hill's *Think and Grow Rich*, and his delivery is second to none!

Find out more here: proctorgallagherinstitute.com

Angi Ponder Reid

How has the Clickety-Clack shown up in your life?

The Clickety-Clack has shown up in my life in three ways:

1. The strongest was a destructive relationship I experienced in my twenties.

2. When I was in my thirties, my dad passed away.

3. In my mid-fifties, my marriage felt like it was falling apart.

The relationship in my twenties was extremely destructive in all areas. There was a lot of drug use and a lot of abuse—physically, sexually, mentally, and emotionally. I began to believe what my abuser said about me, so I became someone who had no idea who I was.

One morning, a friend of mine told me she could no longer be friends with me unless I entered myself into a twelve-step program. I said yes. Once I started the twelve-step program and was aligned with people who had similar stories, I felt a more spiritual connection, now that I was no longer numbing myself with substances. I realized this guy would rather see me dead than with someone else, and the vision of my brain splattered on the wall of the house, and my family finding me dead, was a strong vision.

The next day, I woke up to a voice, speaking to me. I could clearly see Jesus standing in the corner of my bedroom. He held out his hands and said, "Go into the world and prosper."

I said, "Yes."

That day, after my abuser left for work, I called everybody who had a pickup truck. I packed up everything I owned, except my dogs who could not go with me, which broke my heart. I left and I never looked back.

When my dad passed, he was fifty-five years old. We had traveled to Florida on a Monday, and I had this feeling all week long that something bad was going to happen. That Saturday, the phone rang, and I said to myself: *It is my dad.* Yes, it was. He had passed away, unexpectedly. I came home devastated because I was very close to my father, Daddy's little girl. My mom began acting like somebody I did not know.

I said yes to some therapy, and that therapist told me my own expectations were hurting me. Those words stuck with me. Moving forward, I no longer had expectations for my mom because my expectations that she would help me like a mother should were eating me up inside. I needed to allow her to act like a hurt wife.

I experienced marriage troubles in 2016; something did not feel right. I was having a relationship problem with my father-in-law, and when my husband did not have my back on certain issues, I grew resentful. A friend of mine asked me to go to a workshop called *Essence of Being*. I said yes. That workshop is what lead me down the path where I met Keith Leon S. and was asked to be involved in this book project.

How did you navigate the Clickety-Clack?

In my destructive relationship, I had to clean myself up, from the inside out. Then, I got to know myself as an adult. I lived on my own for the first time and learned to respect myself. One of my mottos is: *If I have one foot in yesterday and one foot in tomorrow, I am pissing all over the day I am guaranteed.* I quit looking back, and I quit looking forward. I started living in the present.

Navigating my father's passing took some time because our relationship was so deeply rooted in my being. We were so close; talking about his passing brings up emotions I have not felt in a long time. I learned to see my mom as a hurt little girl and to love her through her loss rather than letting my resentment for her behavior add to my pain.

My marriage troubles and saying yes to Essence of Being led me down a path where I started needing other people. This path is the path of least resistance I have heard Abraham Hicks talk about. My life has happened so smoothly since I went to that first workshop. I went there to gain the courage to get a divorce and live on my own again. After I got home from the three-day workshop, *divorce* was no longer in my vocabulary. I knew I could not give anybody else the power to control my happiness. Happiness was up to me.

Continuing to say yes, I believe the third question is about tools. By saying yes to Essence of Being, I was led to saying yes to more personal development. I found a company that I partnered with, doTERRA. I use these essential oils for emotional benefit, and they have helped me greatly. These choices led me to become a cast member of Awakening Giants, in Ecuador, a part of Brand Builders Club, and a conscious leader with Essence of Being. I have taken The Passion Test and become an *elite* member of the Science of Getting Rich Academy. All these things have been laid on my lap. I did not start this personal development journey as a youngster; I started when I was fifty-four years old.

What tools do you recommend for staying peaceful in a seemingly toxic world?

The first tool I love to use has been staying in alignment. Now, I can feel when I am not. If I am not in alignment, I will not make a decision.

I use my oils during meditation. I used them during this call (to deliver book content) so that I am speaking clearly and my points are spoken as clearly and heartfelt as I can possibly deliver them.

I hold a positive mindset. When I am saying something that does not sound right, I reframe it to make it positive so I am eliminating any resistance or negativity.

I dream *Big*. That is a huge tool for me. When I do not think I can do something, I look back on the times I said yes. Then, I turn my thinking into another dream: *What if? What if?*

I continue to say yes to nudges because when I am in alignment, I receive those nudges clearly. I look forward to something by not *having one foot in yesterday or tomorrow*. If I am looking forward to something, I have learned to count how many trash pickup days will pass until it happens. If it is six weeks from now, I know that is only six trash pickup days. It arrives before I know it because it seems like almost every day the trash is being picked up. This process makes life easier for me.

Knowing when the right things are laid in my lap is such a beautiful feeling because so many things have been brought to me that did not feel right. I know when something is not a yes-nudge because my feelings are my barometer of whether or not I should say yes or no to the next journey or adventure.

I reframe my thoughts. I have felt lonely on a lot of Mother's Days because I did not have children. This past Mother's Day, I learned to reframe what I was feeling to peace. I was feeling the peace a lot of women would like to feel every day of the year. They feel happy and excited to be a mom, but they are feeling honored on just one day.

I quit beating myself up; I have been calling it *lonely*. When I was in that destructive relationship, I thought it was love. After I left the relationship, the drama and the abuse were no longer there. I then thought I was not being loved because I there was no abuse. I learned to reframe that and call it peace.

I had never felt that peace before in my life. So, learning to reframe parts of my life has been beneficial for me.

About the Author

Angi Ponder Reid, CNHP is a passionate Reflexologist, working with clients worldwide. She is the creator of The FLO Technique™ (FLO Feet Love Oils), a certified Essential Oils specialist, the author of *Daily FLO* (to be released), published columnist, and the creator of Aunt G's World Famous Chicken Salad. Reid has accomplished EOB Mastery and is a CLA Graduate, SOGR *elite* Graduate, Awakening Giant cast member, and BBC Mgr. In 1980, she was listed in *Karate Magazine's* Top 10 Martial Arts Legends.

Reid lives in Georgia with her husband, Bill, of twenty-eight years and her two fur-babies, Mork and Mindy. She is a granddaughter to the best grandmother a girl could ever want, and a daughter to parents who, during their own learning experience, raised a curious soul. She is a sister to three *amazing* women who bestowed her with the title "Aunt G" to eighteen nieces and nephews whom she loves dearly.

She is friend to many whom she calls *family*.

Contact info for Angi Ponder Reid:

- feetloveoils@gmail.com
- facebook.com/aponderreid
- Feetloveoils.com

If you can relate to my story or would like to learn more about the tools I use to keep emotional, mental, and physical toxicity at a distance, go to feetloveoils.com and register for my newsletter. You will receive a Free eBook on Essential Oil uses. If you would love to be part of my International DoTERRA team, go to my.doterra.com/feetloveoils.

Donna Riley

How has the Clickety-Clack shown up in your life?

I have actually lived most of life in the Clickety-Clack because I had a near-death experience (NDE) when I was twelve and did not tell anybody for thirty-five years. At the age of forty-seven—I'm now fifty-six—I went through a process where I discovered I was angry about still being on the planet.

Suddenly my whole life started to make sense. I always had a low level of anger and frustration. My mantra was *Nobody gets it* because I knew this three-dimensional reality was an illusion. I have since learned I was responding to life through my trauma. I typically was in a state of fight, flight, or freeze. I was isolated, dissociated, and in fear most of the time. Basically, I wasn't really living because after experiencing pure love and light in my NDE, I didn't want to come fully back into my body.

In the past couple years, I have healed around that experience, and recently, I have decided to follow my truth, trust my intuition, and live fully embodied. For the first time in my life, I recently took the risk of not having a job. Events aligned with this coronavirus pandemic. The studio where I taught was closing, so I started teaching online. As I was teaching online for the studio, I realized: *Wow, this is actually much more in alignment with what I want to create for my life.*

Spirit really spoke loudly that this was the crossroads, this was the opportunity. *It is here. It is time.* Talk about going into the Clickety-Clack! My mind jumped in: *You cannot do this. You do not know what you are doing. You do not know anything about computers, and yet you want to have a business online.* Yet Spirit kept speaking loudly: *Yes, you are going to do this. Yes, this what you are meant to do.*

When you look at the three-dimensional reality of what is happening, this time in the world is pretty scary, and I am actually the calmest and the most centered I have ever been.

How did you navigate the Clickety-Clack?

One of my primary ways I navigate is through movement. I grew up as a dancer, and even though I was not really given the body to be professional, I was happiest when I was moving. When I have gone through stressful or difficult times, my primary method of coping has always been to move. I do not mean specifically dance, but moving as a means to express myself.

If I'm sad, I might be by myself in my home, lying on my mat, rolling around, stretching, and crying. I let movement be the way to express and move things out of me. On the flip side, when I am angry and frustrated, I blast the music and jump around like a lunatic, releasing that energy out of my body because I do not want it there. Then, there are sometimes where I want to feel nurtured, loved, and cared for, so I might lie on the ground with a blanket and candles to enjoy the tranquility of the stillness.

I have discovered there are different aspects of self-care:

- Mental self-care
- Emotional self-care

- Spiritual self-care
- Physical self-care

As I work through my journey, I intentionally practice tools to address all four aspects of myself. For the mental aspect of self-care, I work to keep my mind in the right framework in terms of belief systems. I say mantras to myself every day. Earlier, I spent most of my life constantly criticizing and judging myself.

Now, I intentionally use my strength, will, and presence to say:

- *I am powerful.*
- *I am love.*
- *I am strong.*
- *I am Spirit.*
- *I am God.*

I really *feel* into these statements as I say them. I also catch and stop myself when I say something negative about myself.

For my emotional self-care, I allow emotions to be what they are. I do not judge them; I do not criticize them. I let them flow through me and I honor them. I know I am receiving a message if something makes me sad or excited. I listen, pay attention, and honor each emotion without judging it.

For physical self-care, I practice mindful movement, eating well, drinking lots of water, and getting quality sleep.

In the spiritual realm, I joke and say I have spent most of my life in the light. It was my escapism to leave my body and go to the light, like my NDE. Now, my practice spiritually is to embody the connection of heaven and Earth. I understand that connecting to light is leaving, and while it is wonderful, I need to bring that light into my body, come back and be here, and then carry it forth as I interact with others.

What tools do you recommend for staying peaceful in a seemingly toxic world?

My number one tool is movement, staying present in my body. I encourage practicing mantras. One of the simplest yet most powerful ones I use is: *In this moment, I am safe and okay.*

I recommend a daily practice that focuses on going within and connecting to Source. I do not think it is only sitting and meditating; it can be going for a walk and staying present to the awe-inspiring beauty of Mother Earth. Nature speaks to me. When you are in the presence of nature, I highly encourage you to look around and listen. The trees talk to me. For you, it might be something different. It might be the water; it might be the ground or the earth that has a message for you, that wants to connect with you or support you in some way.

Nature reminds us of the cycles of death and rebirth. The leaves fall from the trees, and as they decompose, they become part of the earth where new seeds will be planted. They turn into compost that turns into earth. This rich earth fertilizes new roots and new growth. There is always death and rebirth. There is always renewal. Pay attention when you are in nature to the cycles, the lessons, the teachings, and the wisdom there for you if you stay present.

I encourage dreaming and visualizing. Give yourself the precious gift of dreaming even though you might feel completely overwhelmed with stress and fear, with things that you believe will hurt you.

If you had your ideal life, if you could create anything, what would it look like? How would you feel?

The mind does not know the difference between what you are imagining and what you are actually doing. Spend time in the world of creating and dreaming and allow yourself to focus on those dreams every day.

Finally, take if from a girl who's been to the Light. Remember everything has a divine purpose. Stay in love, stay in gratitude, stay in faith.

About the Author

Donna Riley is a gifted intuitive movement teacher and inner transformation leader. She knows her purpose is to awaken, inspire, and empower women to alchemize their pain into pleasure. This is a deeply personal mission for Donna because after having a Near Death Experience at the age of twelve, she has spent the rest of her life learning how to be fully embodied and to enjoy this three-dimensional world. For the past thirty years, Donna has studied movement science, energy medicine, personal development, epigenetics, and other healing modalities. She uses the tools of Pilates, primal movement, fascia release, breathwork, and meditation while following the guidance of the messages she receives as to what is needed for her client at that time. Her programs and private sessions facilitate experiences in which the client learns to listen to the divine intelligence of their body, move with grace and fire, and create an orgasmic life.

If you would like to learn more about my work and receive a free video on how to feel amazing in your body, email me at orgasmicmovement@gmail.com.

Deborah Robbins

How has the Clickety-Clack shown up in your life?

Have you ever heard *things come in threes?*

In September of 2014, my life was at an all-time high. I lived in a condo on a beach in Florida, and I stayed fit by walking, running, and practicing hot yoga. I was serving in a member- and industry-relations leadership role for a nonprofit organization, where I managed a nine-state territory on the other side of the country. I traveled frequently and had ongoing communications with thousands of industry workers, business professionals, educators, and students. I regularly spoke at professional meetings and participated in industry events all over the country. Life was good.

After returning home from a successful business trip on a Wednesday night, I was awakened on Thursday morning by a phone call from one of my sisters. She was calling to tell me the devastating news that our mother had been killed, and our nephew severely injured, in a car accident.

Mother was the most kind, unconditionally loving, caring, generous, encouraging, and inspiring person and believer I have ever known. She was also my best friend. My rock. My counselor and confidante. She had been the wind beneath my wings throughout my life. According to her, every day was the best day of her life. And she was gone.

The next few days were surreal. I thank God for our friends and community who loved our family through a very difficult week and the many challenging days that followed.

I began feeling extreme pain in my stomach area, and I thought it was probably due to emotional stress related to all the trauma. Then, I started throwing up in shades of green I had never seen. I was taken to a nearby hospital where, after a few hours of testing, I was admitted for further evaluation.

After several days of additional testing, scanning, and consulting with many doctors, I was told there was an inoperable aneurysm on my common hepatic artery, and that I was going to die. The diagnosis was incomprehensible. I was being referred to a top-rated hospital for specialized care.

Just a few days before, I was happy and healthy, living a full, productive, and prosperous life. Then, Mother was gone, my young nephew was recovering from major surgery required by his injuries sustained in the accident, and I was told that I was going to die.

The following week, we received news that our first grandchild was in her mother's womb. That glorious confirmation of new life was delivered to us with perfect timing.

In the coming weeks, I saw specialized doctors who confirmed the diagnosis I had been given. Although they showed me visual evidence, I did not believe it. In addition to the medicines that would support my body in healing, my treatment plan included a new daily life plan.

All my normal activity was stopped to prevent the aneurysm from rupturing. All my projects and plans were put on hold for, hopefully, only four months. No exercise, no travel, no stress, no worry. No excitement of any kind. I was instructed to *simply be* and allow the healing to happen.

My new daily routine was to wake up, brush my teeth, and shower. That's all. Some days, it was a challenge to do all three. My mind was always searching for answers. At times, I wished it would stop. The grief of loss, the disbelief of the diagnosis, and the pain of uncertainty, in addition to the joyful news about our first grandchild, was overwhelming.

I was hopeful and heartbroken. Happy and sad. I felt blessed and yet miserably incapable of being of value to our family at that time. The life-saving medicines I was taking caused temporary health issues, and I was a mess. On some days, I was barely hanging on.

How did you navigate the Clickety-Clack?

> *Leaders inspire others only to the point*
> *they inspire themselves.*
> *You cannot give what you do not have.*
> ~ John Maxwell

I prayed and I asked everyone to pray. I sat and pondered the miracle of life and the purpose of life. Then, I prayed more. I felt gratitude and I felt grief. I felt pain and anger, and I am not an angry person. In fact, I have been told I can be annoyingly positive and optimistic.

Then, I started to feel better. As the days passed through mindless fog, I felt a blanket of love wrap around me. I knew the prayers were being heard, and I knew everything was going to be all right. By taking it one day at a time, I had a renewed passion for living, healing, and being as healthy as I could be going forward. I was going to be a grandmother.

I began researching every topic that came to mind. Since my calendar was cleared, I had plenty of time. As the weeks passed, I researched for ten to fourteen hours every day. I read and studied potential ways to improve various areas of my life—health, emotions, eating, spirituality, physical, financial, and fun.

Then I started participating virtually—online and via phone—with new people and new groups of people. These connections were important lifelines for me; they were my main source of contact with the outside world.

Utilizing emotional intelligence trainings and essential oils became two of my top interests. Both presented new options for taking care of myself and my family using natural, proven methods. I was captivated by the amount of information available on the importance of managing our emotions in order to maintain healthy lives. I was impressed by the quantity and quality of essential oils, and the benefits that could be realized by using them for support with physical, mental, emotional, and spiritual issues.

The more I learned, the more I wanted to learn, and the more I wanted to share what I learned to help others.

At my four-month checkup, the doctors told me *the aneurysm was gone.* The scans showed that the area where it had previously presented was healed and appeared normal. They said it was as if *a healing miracle had occurred.*

My new life plan was to *live* without restrictions, to *share* all that I had learned, and to *assist* others with improving their lives and reaching their well-being potential.

I felt empowered and overjoyed to let my light shine again.

What tools do you recommend for staying peaceful in a seemingly toxic world?

By the time you read this, six years will have passed. I remain healed, thank God.

In retrospect, I believe stress and a lack of prioritizing my own well-being caused the aneurysm diagnosis. I continue to study, utilize, and promote emotional intelligence trainings. I also love discovering and sharing new ways to use essential oils in caring for my family, myself, and others.

I meditate, journal, and exercise regularly. I eat healthfully. I allow my inner child to play with our granddaughters as often as possible. I am mindful about seeing the good in every situation and about keeping my emotional frequency high.

My advice for staying in a peaceful state of mind:

- *Breathe*—deeply and slowly.

- Exercise your faith.

- Don't take stuff personally.

- Stay in action and trust your inner knowing.

- Live in the present. Look for the good in every experience.

- Be empathetic, able to see situations from another's point of view.

- Remain open-minded. Find ways to love others through differences of opinion.

- Love and respect yourself.

- Discover your personal values, so you may know and live your purpose.

- Feel gratitude and write about what you are grateful for. Writing is a game changer.

- Seek clarity about what you want, then stay focused and pursue it.

- Be curious and creative. Learn something new every day.

- Collaborate and create with others. Compare to and compete with yourself only.

- Remember you always have a choice about how you feel.

- Use memories, but don't allow memories to use you.

- Use *afformations*—intensions framed as questions. Ask and it is given.

- Believe you can be, do, or have anything.

- Life is a journey with many destinations. Decide to enjoy every one of them.

- Surround yourself with like-minded people, even virtually.

- We are a combination of the five people we spend the most time with. Choose wisely.

- Be mindful about how the power of your thoughts, words, and actions.

- Appreciate that everything is temporary. Be at peace with change, the only constant.

- Let your personal light shine. Share a smile, a kind word, or a good deed simply because you can.

- Understand that giving and receiving are the same energy. The more you give, the more you receive. The more you receive, the more you can give.

About the Author

Embrace life like a child.

Deborah Robbins is a dynamic businesswoman, bestselling author, speaker, and published columnist. She earned a bachelor's degree in marketing and management and has several professional certifications. She engages and connects people so they can strategically optimize opportunities.

Throughout her career, Deborah has served various industries in leadership roles within human resources and benefits administration, marketing and sales, project and product management, business and territory development, non-profit organizations, and directing new facility startups.

She utilizes her skills, knowledge, and extensive networks to educate and inspire about the relevance of modern-day manufacturing, innovative thinking, and the power of personal choices.

Since her wake-up call in 2014, Deborah has earnestly studied and applied emotional intelligence training and essential oil practices to maximize her mental, physical, emotional, and spiritual health.

She is an advocate for well-being with a passion for gratitude, leadership, mindfulness, and choosing to be happy.

Deborah believes in *The One Philosophy*—we are all connected. She is dedicated to assisting others realize their potential to achieve their desired outcomes. You may contact Deborah for tips, tools, and valuable resources at: DeborahRobbinsXS@gmail.com.

Jani Roberts

How has the Clickety-Clack shown up in your life?

My first answer to that question reflects a strong desire from childhood. When I was a little girl, I was extremely connected. My grandmother was connected to Source, and we had a powerful bond. From an early age, I felt connected to the trees, to the sky, to my family, to animals, and to Source. There was no doubt in my mind that life was beautiful and amazing.

I knew this when I rode my pony, when I went sledding in our backyard, rolled down the hill into a pile of leaves, and walked through the forest to my Gram's house. I was so connected to all this, I thought to myself: *This is where I should be. This is the right time for me.* I could feel the trees breathing, and I knew *God is good.* I knew it in my heart.

While my heart held these beliefs, I began unlearning many powerful truths as I grew up. I paid attention to what other people said, what they thought and believed in. I did not really understand why their beliefs were important to me. No one told me it mattered; it just seemed like it should. To be honest, I did not connect well with people. I connected more easily with animals; they were much easier to talk to, and their unconditional love was always present, even when I wasn't patient.

149

My story has taken many turns, as I am sure yours has as well. It has been amazing, horrible, fantastic, and miserable. It has been painful. It has been lonely and also full of love. It has come full circle. I have finally reconnected, and this connection is my desire for all. I remember who I am now, a little girl trying to figure it out and have as much fun as possible. Through this process, I have found that my patterns of behavior created beliefs. Some have served me, some not so much.

Perhaps, you have felt this way too?

It is good to know what you do not want or like as that knowledge brings you closer to understanding what does feel right. I truly believe the Universe loves me and knows my heart. I believe this to be true for each of us.

I have not made mistakes nor has anyone else. That can be a hard truth to swallow because it leaves us with no one to blame. Each of us is doing the best we can with the tools we are given. Each day I work to build new beliefs. Everyone can do this: change patterns, find new ways of thinking, care less about what others think, and focus more on how they feel.

Remember to mind your own business and do your own work. Treat others as you like to be treated. This is my promise. When I get my feet stuck in the mud, I will do what I need to do, even if it means leaving shoes behind. I believe you will too. We will work this practice together, learn to quiet our minds and listen. Just try. That will be enough.

It is time for a new story for all of us. Now is the time for your story. Let your story become your path to follow, to build, to reconnect, and to find your way. You have made no mistakes.

Have as much fun as possible and always remember: *We are in this together.*

How did you navigate the Clickety-Clack?

The most powerful tool I found when I was navigating the Clickety-Clack is a quiet mind. I was quite the hyper child.

We all pick up beliefs about ourselves along the way:

- We are too hyper; we are too calm.
- We are too lazy; we work too hard.
- We are too short; we are too tall.
- We are too fat; we are too thin.
- We are too smart; we are not smart enough.

I practice feeling my way through all these beliefs. *Does that feel true for me? or Does that feel untrue?* As a child, it is easy; it is a kind of yucky-or-yummy theory. If it felt good, it was yummy, and if it did not, it was yucky. Why would anyone want to hang out in yucky when there is so much yummy? I would bask in good-feeling places and avoid the places that felt not-so-good.

This practice led me on a journey to develop more patterns of behavior. One pattern for me was hiding. I would hide when things did not feel good. I would move away from them, but I was not always sure about where I should move. For many years, I was moving away, moving away, moving away. As that pattern became not-so-good feeling, I found tools like meditation and movement that helped me find freedom in my safe space, freedom in my mind.

I learned quickly the only thing I could control were my thoughts. Whatever felt good is what I leaned toward. You may have experienced this, and this leaning can take you on a variety of paths. It could take you down a relief path of addictions—anything from substance, shopping, hoarding, or hiding. These are simply distractions to avoid facing what needs to be addressed. Addressing our thoughts is our work. In order to find joy, we must find our way through these distractions.

So, as I bobbed and weaved, I found many mentors, many teachers. You will find them. Perhaps you have found one here. You have had people come into your life to teach you, even if it was not frequently. You remember who they were—the people of empowerment. These people spoke words of truth that resonated with you. They always put a smile on your face when you think of them. They may not have been a dominating presence in your life, but you were aligned. You attracted them into your experience so they would remind you of who you really are.

This was true for me. I attracted mentors into my experiences, and I clung closely to them, to learn. I hung on their words. I took them into my heart, and I sat with them. I paid attention to how they made me feel. I knew I wanted more of that.

Don't you?

I am sure you can relate when you find yourself sitting in what feels good.

Why not bask in it? Why not sit there longer?

Why not pay attention to how you feel and remind yourself this is what you want to be feeling most of the time?

You are going to experience some of the not-so-good feeling stuff, but spend most of your time in these better-feeling places and look for mentors. Keep an eye out for those teachers. They will come. You can attract them in whatever way or whatever time you need them to arrive into your experience.

What tools do you recommend for staying peaceful in a seemingly toxic world?

Well, breath is key. I need to take a deep breath after hearing the question. I am sure you feel the need to take a deep breath because it is easy to shut down in a seemingly toxic world. But we know the truth; there is more good than not. It is, very simply, a choice.

What do we choose to give our attention to?

During this process, I actually created a practice from all the different work I have experienced over the course of my life. I have spent fifty-plus years working a practice of connection, peace, prosperity, and contentment, because I knew I needed tools.

One of the key tools I use is *Alignment Essentials' School of Unlearning*. It is a 365-day course developed as a result of my need to put all my tools in a space that would help me. In this course, you can create more of what you want and less of what you don't want. I needed a practice that I could do anytime, anywhere. This practice asks for just a few minutes of time each day.

It will teach you how to quiet your mind. I know it can seem difficult, particularly in a seemingly toxic world. A quiet mind is the key to peace. You do not need to do this aggressively; you need to do this breath by breath, word by word, thought by thought, belief by belief. Once you begin a simple daily practice, you open the pathways for additional mentors. This path will lead you to books that will be life-changing. You have already experienced this in your lifetime, in this time and space. You have already connected with certain works that blew your mind. There is so much more out there.

You have a purpose. We're all born with one. We arrive on fire with our purpose. At first, it is vague yet powerful. Mine was rough and a bit coarse. It had a mind of its own and took me on an amazing journey, as will yours. I struggled to find my place. Everyone was ready to tell me what to do. I tried to listen. They didn't have the answers. Their advice was not all poorly intended, but mostly, it was.

Can you relate?

I had to enroll in my own *School of Unlearning*. I had to find my way home, to live in alignment through hurdle after hurdle. Your mind's purpose is to protect you, to make sure you survive the hurdles. You will. It's all about unlearning the untruths, reconnecting, and starting over.

Contrast will serve you well. You must know hot to know cold, know fear to know peace, experience anger to appreciate love, and find your purpose to find your freedom. Suddenly, the world will seem not toxic at all.

About the Author

Jani Roberts is the Co-Founder and Co-CEO of Alignment Essentials, a health and wellness company spanning the fitness, self-improvement, and mindfulness spaces. She is the creator of all Alignment Essentials programming content. Jani is also the co-host of the podcast, *Inspirational Conversations for Living in Alignment*.

Jani has over forty years of experience in the health and wellness field. Before launching her own brand in 2011, Jani was a master trainer for a world-renowned fitness format where she trained hundreds of thousands of teachers internationally. Jani is a graduate of the American Academy of Nutrition, and presenter for IDEA, SCW, Rimini, IHRSA, CAN FIT PRO, AAAI, Lifetime EMPOWER Events, Club Industry, FILEX, FIBO, Nike, and Adidas. She holds certifications from ACE, AFAA and NASM.

Jani travels extensively as a speaker, author, and presenter, sharing her Alignment Essentials wellness tools and helping people find more joy in their lives.

For a free gift, go to alignmentessentails.com/bookgift.

Trisha Schmalhofer

How has the Clickety-Clack shown up in your life?

We are multidimensional beings, so there is always an aspect of us in the Clickety-Clack, always in an adjustment period, somewhere. I have had many times in my life that were really big Clickety-Clack moments.

The one that I want to share is my mother's death and passing, which was a huge Clickety-Clack. She had a form of dementia called *Lewy body dementia* that was progressive. She declined quickly over a period of time. That whole period was the Clickety-Clack of our family adjusting to her condition and me adjusting my relationship with her.

I believe we are always in a state of flux, and I do not think I have ever been fully in balance. I am sensitive and aware of all these different aspects of myself and others in the world. It has been a journey, learning to navigate through that flux on a continual basis. I find my balance based on where I am in my life and what is going on. Sometimes I find the balance by dancing, singing, and being with friends. Sometimes, when the Clickety-Clack shows up, I find my balance by meditating, resting more, being quiet, connecting with nature, and contemplating.

My mother was my portal into this world. Her passing is probably the biggest Clickety-Clack I have experienced. When she left, I become aware that my entrance door was gone. She was my door into this world; I came through her. What a profound experience that was for me, a deeply spiritual experience. So, the Clickety-Clack of her death, my family navigating it, and the realization that my entryway into this realm was now gone changed the way I connected to God.

So far in my life, my mother's death was the biggest Clickety-Clack in the midst of smaller- and medium-sized Clickety-Clacks.

How did you navigate the Clickety-Clack?

I navigated the Clickety-Clack by staying connected to:

- My Higher Power
- My Higher Self
- My body
- My mind
- My spirit
- My family
- Friends
- Nature

We got the call telling us the nurses were seeing signs that she was passing, and I flew to Pennsylvania. Before this, we had made plans for how it was going to be. Once we arrived, I stayed the night by her side, giving her healing and trying to make her comfortable. The next day, we met with hospice and made plans for her passing. A harpist was going to come and play. We were sitting around the table with the hospice nurse, planning what we could, and I said, "Has everyone told Mom what they need to tell her and said goodbye?"

Everyone except for my dad said yes, and we let him know it was important for her to know it was okay to go. That same night, when she started going and her breathing changed, I texted my brother. Earlier, he decided he was not going to come back to the nursing home that night, but he was already on his way. Something told him to be there. All her children and her husband were there. I got on the phone and texted the rest of my family, including her sister and some of my friends, that she was leaving this planet at that moment.

Having them energetically connect to us at that time formed a profound energetic, peaceful, loving grid for my mom to pass through. I connected with her angels, with her guides, with God. We were praying. My sister was at her head; I was at her feet. The rest of the family was around her. I had studied shamanic practices and Catholic rituals to assist her to fully leave her body. I had the psychic gift to see the tunnel of light prepared for her, a pathway. We were all present and in this flow. We were touching her; we were talking to her. We told my father to let her go and he did. As soon as he said the words, she passed.

Then of course, he said, "No, I do not mean it."

He had his own process, but he had already spoken the words. She passed. Here is the most profound thing: I felt her after she was legally dead while there was still activity in her brain, still a craniosacral rhythm. There was still an energy field. For twenty to twenty-five minutes, I could feel my mother's body that was *dead* and *not dead*. My sister, brother, and I sat and told stories and laughed as I felt every spark leave and calm down until the last spark flickered in the center of her brain.

When we are legally dead, we are not. Then, there was a shamanic Earth-based energy exchange that happened after I felt that last spark leave her brain. There was a collection of energy left in her body going back into the Earth.

Navigating the Clickety-Clack by being in the flow allowed me, my brother, and my sister to share and feel what was happening with my mom after she was legally dead. That experience was a sacred gift.

What tools do you recommend for staying peaceful in a seemingly toxic world?

The tools that I recommend:

1. Self-awareness
2. Compassion
3. Connection
4. Breathing
5. Exploration
6. Expression

The first tool is being **self-aware** enough to know you are in the Clickety-Clack. Be aware of what is happening in your physical body, mental body, emotions, and where you are in space and time.

My second tool is **compassion** for yourself and other people. We are all in this together, and we are all pretty much going through the Clickety-Clack at any given time. We are all living this life, and it is not always easy. So, have compassion and remember we are all human.

The third tool is to **connect** and communicate in any way you can. Talk to some trees. Talk to some butterflies. Talk to some family members who are balanced. Connect with God or a higher power. Connect with your higher self or your angels or your guides. When you are in the midst of toxicity, connect with what feeds you and gives you peace, joy, and love.

Another tool is **breathing**. It is a simple thing. Breath brings Spirit into your body. Inspiration means to bring Spirit in, which will center you and bring clarity. It does not need to be fancy breathing. Even simple breath will focus you and bring you into that divine center within your heart space.

The next tool is **exploring**. Have fun finding what brings you joy and inner peace. It changes sometimes so you might find new things:

- A new song
- A new dance
- A new form of meditation
- A new way of moving
- A new discipline or practice
- A new religion or spiritual structure
- A new place in nature you have not visited before

Explore what is filling you up and bringing you peace. Have fun doing it.

Isn't that why we are here? To love and have fun?

The last tool is **expressing** and allowing whatever emotion is coming up. Acknowledging feelings is like self-awareness:

Hey, I am feeling kind of down and depressed today. Allow that. Sometimes you need to experience the feeling for a little while, and then let it move through you and transition out. Then, you can explore balance or acknowledge you are having a really good day even if everyone is not. And that it is okay. Allow yourself to be joyful in the midst of other people's misery. You do not have to match their vibration. Express exactly where you are at any time.

About the Author

Trisha Schmalhofer is an alchemist of the Soul, whisperer of the body, and channel for Divine wisdom. Her passion and expertise for blending the structure of science with the flow of Spirit has created a successful career as a MedHealers Licensed Integrative Healer, Akashic Records Specialist, and Master Intuitive for over twenty-two years. Her personal insights into spiritual authenticity helped catapult her book, *The Beauty of Authenticity* to number one Amazon Bestseller status.

As creator and hostess of the far-reaching podcast *BAM—Badasses, Alchemists, Mystics,* Trisha features awe-inspiring guests who ignite change in the world by sharing their genuine badass selves. After just one year, the successful *BAM* podcast is embraced on multiple platforms including Facebook, YouTube, and all Space Coast Podcast Network outlets. Trisha's most recent alchemical success, the BAM Community, blends livestreamed classes, retreats, and events in nature that empower people to embrace their inner BAM and live their most inspired lives.

Since connection to our higher selves is so important during the Clickety-Clacks of life, here is a Free Gift from Trisha Schmalhofer: *10 Steps to Connect with Your Higher Self,* medhealers.com/gift.

While on her website, please subscribe to the MedHealers/ BAM Community email list on the pop-up window or contact page, so you stay updated on all mystical, alchemical badassery. Email questions or insight to bamcommunity11@gmail.com.

Venetta Stathis

How has the Clickety-Clack shown up in your life?

The Clickety-Clack has been a part of my life since I was very young. I was raised as a Greek Orthodox Christian—very traditional, orthodox, staunch Christian. I call it the Bible-box way to live. There were not many shades of gray. If we asked about our traditions and why we did certain things, we were told *because that is how we were taught.* That is what Greeks do. That is what our culture says. I was raised without much leeway in how I lived my life and what I wanted to do.

My spirit was on a different plane, my spirit was a rebel, and my spirit wanted to know answers. My spirit did not always believe what I had been taught. I married when I was seventeen, like good Greek girls did back in that day. I had a son, but the marriage was not a good marriage and I divorced, which was totally unheard of in the church and the Orthodox community. Predominantly, Greek girls did not divorce.

I was a single mom for probably fifteen years when I was presented with a guy my family wanted me to marry. Of course, Greek girls get married, that is what they do. I was entering the golden years at the ripe old age of thirty-five, and they were certain I *should* want a companion. I did remarry. With that marriage, I somehow conformed and started living everything I had rebelled against. I became a good Greek wife.

I was haunted by the spirits of my ancestors: *Greek girls do this. Greek girls do that.* I conformed and put my spirit to bed. I had always been the noncomformist of the family. My entire family married and had their children. I was the single mom out there doing the things Greek women did not do. Greek women conformed—they stayed home and were good housekeepers and wives. Because I was a single mom, I had to be a working girl.

That was my Clickety-Clack. *Which side did I belong on? Did I belong on the spirituality side? Did I belong on the Orthodox side? Where did I fit?* There was a constant turmoil in my brain: *Where do I fit? Who am I? Do I be who I am or do I conform and become who they want me to be?*

How did you navigate the Clickety-Clack?

In 1996, I moved to Greece with my husband. I was a good Greek wife and was determined this second marriage was going to work, whether it was a good one or not. It was a horrible marriage. If I did not love Greece so much, I do not know if I would have stayed with him, but I did stay. In 2008, I saw a YouTube video about how to know if you are a lightworker, and that video woke up something within me.

Then, someone gave me a copy of *The Secret* by Rhonda Byrne (Atria, 2006), but this copy had Abraham-Hicks in it. I began following Abraham-Hicks. I was introduced somewhere along the way to Doreen Virtue. I had a holistic doctor in Greece, and I became good friends with one of her patients. One of her best friends was a woman who painted icons, iconography. She spoke to angels. The icons she painted were channeled by these angels and put on canvas.

I was very excited. It was a whole new world I knew nothing about. I say I did not know anything about it, but I did know a lot about it because part of my struggle in the early days was that within myself I knew things I did not know I knew. I started to play on social media sites. I lived in Greece and had to speak Greek all the time. It was fun playing with Americans with whom I was able to speak English.

I fell in love with an *enigma*. I never saw him. I called him *my defibrillator*. We only communicated online, but he woke up the spiritual side of me, my spirit whom I had tucked safely away for many years. That spirit began guiding me in a different direction. I felt calmer. I knew more about what I wanted and where I should be. Somehow, the guilt started leaving, and I was on my way to becoming who I was or who I was supposed to be.

What tools do you recommend for staying peaceful in a seemingly toxic world?

After I made my decision to leave Greece, I came home. Although I enjoyed many of the speakers from *The Secret* (Atria, 2006), it was Abraham-Hicks who spoke to my heart, so I continued to follow him. I began following Mike Dooley. I did more work with Doreen Virtue. I had always been an essential oil user but it was because they were predominately natural and I was more of a natural girl. I did not realize the emotional healing aspects of oils.

I learned about oils and crystals. I began studying Reiki. I connected to Nature's soul.

*All man needs for good health and
healing can be found in nature.*
~ Paracelsus, father of pharmacology

Crystals, Reiki, energy. These three important things speak to me. Returning to nature and connecting with the soul of nature will bring you peace. You connect with the heavens; you connect with the Earth. Our Father lives in heaven; the Earth is our Mother. You live between two loving parents. If you can tap into that energy, it will bring you peace and well-being.

I love Janet Bray Attwood. I do not follow her as much, but I have a connection with her I absolutely love. I try to watch as many of her videos as possible. I enjoy her chants and was introduced to Snatam Kaur, a New Age devotional musician and peace activist. Her music is calming, and when the Clickety-Clack begins, I navigate myself to her music.

I enjoy meditations. There are meditations based on frequencies, called Solfeggio frequencies, or vibrations in musical tones. Those are calming meditations.

There is an alternate nostril breathing exercise I learned from Janet:

1. Hold the left nostril closed
2. Inhale through the right nostril
3. Release the left nostril and hold the right nostril closed
4. Exhale out the left nostril and inhale through the left nostril
5. Release the right nostril and hold the left nostril closed
6. Exhale out the right nostril and inhale through the right nostril
7. Repeat several times

If you do that for several moments, you will experience calmness and peace. It is amazing.

The mantra I live my life by is *living in the moment.* One of my favorite sayings is: *Trust and allow, and do not ask how.*

If you learn to trust, if you live your life in love, and if you stop trying to figure out the cursed *hows,* you will arrive at a place of calmness, a place of acceptance, and a place of living in the moment. Whatever tomorrow brings, you will have the wherewithal to deal with it.

About the Author

It brings me great joy to share my gifts and help humanity create a happy, healthy life. My name is Venetta. I am a gypsy at heart and a believer in life's magic. The simple things in life make my heart soar: walking the beach, scrunching the sand between my toes, listening to the sound of the waves breaking on the shore; drinking a cup of coffee in the park with a friend; sitting in a garden with a glass of wine, enjoying nature and connecting to God. I believe in the fairies of the universe, that we should love, that we should live life passionately, and that, with a click of our heels, anything is possible. Above all, I believe by connecting with the gifts of Mother Earth and the Universe, we find love and *that* is what brings us peace and joy.

Visit venettastathis.com.

Christy Whitman

How has the Clickety-Clack shown up in your life?

The Clickety-Clack has shown up in different aspects of my life when there is a transition point happening from moment to moment. Some transition points for me were going through a divorce, moving from the States to Canada, going through points and processes in my business, and my newborn son undergoing heart surgery. I went through the healing process after my sister committed suicide. I did not know where I was going in all these aspects of my life; I did not have certainty. I could not see the path in front of me.

I would describe the Clickety-Clack as being *Jane of the Jungle,* going through life, grabbing the next vine in front of me, reaching for the next vine, and finding the vine is not there. I needed to let go of the vine or swing back into the cliff, right? I had to let go even though I could not see the vine in front of me. Even when I fell down—what appeared to be a fall down—something always caught me.

That moment of the Clickety-Clack, where I was not quite out of transition, has been about having, developing, and strengthening a sense of faith—faith in what I wanted. I was deliberate in focusing on what I wanted versus letting my mind take me in the direction of catastrophic possibilities. I have been in trouble

173

financially, in and out of debt, wondering: *Where is the payment going to come from? How am I going to get out of this?*

Absolute fear and terror would arise, and I could not sleep; I was feeling confused and foggy, with no clear way or direction. When I started applying the universal laws, practicing having faith, and focusing on what I wanted, the Clickety-Clack became an easier process. I kept asking myself: *Why do I want it? How do I want to feel?*

How did you navigate the Clickety-Clack?

1. Having a coach has been absolutely essential. I need someone who can see a different perspective. A mentor, an energy healer, or a coach helps me see where I am and where I want to go. I am so grateful that I can be that person for a lot of people. I am privileged to be a coach that helps people out of the Clickety-Clack because it is so rewarding. Having a coach is one of the reasons I have successfully and elegantly moved through the uncertainty of the Clickety-Clack in different, scary parts of my life.

2. Having my own spiritual meditative practice was absolutely essential. I closed my eyes and felt my divine self—energy-wise—telling me: *It is going to be okay.* I felt a sense of being connected to the energy of what I wanted, feeling it first as an energetic reality. That feeling allowed the transition point to be less scary.

3. Knowing about the universal laws allowed me to move toward what I wanted instead of being stuck in whatever was preventing my progress at the time. I knew that whatever contrasts I was experiencing in my life, I could have a moment of deliberate intent, saying what I wanted instead, and then, I would feel the energy flowing toward that reality.

Those three things: having a coach, having my own spiritual connection to my divine, and knowing how to navigate the universal laws and deliberately focus have all been essential in navigating through the Clickety-Clacks of my life.

All of us have these abilities:

- We can hire a coach because there are so many coaches now; it is not as if we cannot find one.

- We can attract support to ourselves; all of us have the ability to do that.

- We can connect with our divine self because it is always within us, breathing us.

- We can engage the universal laws, especially the seven essential laws, whether we know it or not.

I found out about the universal laws twenty-five years ago. I had to dig and search. Now, you just ask Google on the computer, and it pops up. Everything is so easy, so much easier and accessible because people like Keith Leon S. and me have dug through the trenches so more people could have this information.

What tools do you recommend for staying peaceful in a seemingly toxic world?

From quantum physics and modern science, we know everything is energy, including our emotions.

By exercising our free will, we have control of five things:

1. What we say
2. What we think
3. What we believe, or the perspective that we hold
4. What we feel, our emotions
5. What we do

Those are the five elements of being an energy master. We cannot control what is happening outside of us, but we have the ability to choose. Every one of us has free will and choice. In any moment, we can choose to flow in the energy of peace, abundance, or success—or whatever we want to experience. Most of us think we can't feel what we want until the outer circumstances change, until we get that relationship, or until we have a certain level of success. The truth is we need to feel first, and then what we want becomes our experience.

Even though things might seem like they are spinning out of control outside us, we choose to take the only control we have, which is attuning our energy to what we want. We can start each morning by saying: *I choose to feel joy today.* We can imagine we are being filled with joyful energy, and our trillion cells that have receptor sites will be filled with the energy of joy.

As we move about our day, we do not take one sip of water and are then done drinking water for the day. We fill ourselves up and refresh ourselves all day long. We fuel ourselves with food all day long. We eliminate wastes all day long. We are physical beings, but we are also energy beings. We need to fill ourselves, refuel ourselves, and refill ourselves with the energy we want.

If we are not doing that deliberately, our receptor cells will pick up all the energy out there from social media, the news, energy in the airwaves, and our neighbors, and we will be influenced by it. When we are deliberate and choose the energy we want to be filled with, the other energy around us is transmuted in our presence because our receptor sites are already filled with the energy we chose.

When we are choosing to be at peace with our energy, we focus our minds on:

- Thoughts of peace
- What we want
- How we want to experience life
- What we look forward to
- What we appreciate

Then, our emotions feel good because we are in alignment with abundance. Lack always feels bad, and abundance always feels good. As long as we are in alignment with abundance, we can be at peace and feel good amid anything happening in our outer reality. Work with energy. Become an energy master.

About the Author

Christy Whitman is the channel for The Council, spiritual mentors here to spread the message of Quantum Energy Mastery. Christy and The Council teach classes and meditations and provide private sessions to help clients feel more aligned with their Divine Design of well-being, abundance, success, and loving and supportive relationships.

For over fifteen years, and before channeling The Council, Christy was a Transformational Leader, Celebrity Coach, and Law of Attraction expert, as well as the two-time *New York Times* bestselling author of *The Art of Having It All and Taming Your Alpha Bitch.*

Christy has appeared on the news, *The Today Show, The Morning Show,* Ted X, and The Hallmark Channel. Her work has been featured in various media publications. She's been featured in *Goalcast, People Magazine, Seventeen, Woman's Day, Hollywood Life,* and *Teen Vogue,* to name a few.

Learn more about Christy here: ChristyWhitman.com.

Lea Williamson

How has the Clickety-Clack shown up in your life?

Most recently, the Clickety-Clack showed up, as it has for a lot of people, in the COVID-19 situation. That's been quite an unexpected wave to ride. It came from nowhere—for pretty much everyone. Personally, it's impacted me in a lot of ways. My work stopped for about three months from the shutdowns. The business where I worked over three years closed their doors permanently and is no longer an option. My indoor tai chi and qigong classes stopped altogether.

Fortunately, I have been teaching outdoors for many years in the parks where I live. I was able to continue leading those classes for healthy people who are willing to come out. Here in Florida, my classes in the public parks fell under the governor's *essential services* definition during the shutdowns. The healing power of nature and community was welcomed by those who came. I am grateful they chose to keep themselves healthy.

The COVID Clickety-Clack also showed up in the panic and fear it brought into my world in ways I never expected. My typically rock-solid dad was shaken into stress mode. My dad never panics, never fears. When he did, his panic and fear affected me. That was the only significant time I was affected by

181

the wave of fear and stress that COVID brought, and I was able to manage it fairly well.

The combination of the loss of my church community and the loss of my dad's stability left me feeling cut off from others. Add the lack of interaction from working less, and I recognized my need for community more than ever.

Being a touch-oriented person, physical distancing has also affected me. Not being able to hug people has affected my physical body in unexpected ways. During our first month of quarantine, I longed for touch so much, I started hugging trees.

While there have been many times the Clickety-Clack has shown up in my life, this one has definitely been the biggest test of my self-management because of the multiple ways I've been affected:

- Financial insecurity and with it, housing insecurity
- Security blanket of a parent taken away
- Loss of community with my church shutting down
- No touch whatsoever in my touch-oriented life

This has been the roughest wave I've ever had to ride, without a doubt.

How did you navigate the Clickety-Clack?

I've ridden this wave pretty well. I see other people reacting irrationally in some ways, and by comparison, I'm doing just fine. I only had one panic moment, when my dad freaked me out. In a sense, I was prepared for it because of my normal daily life. As soon as I realized that it was the spread of false information that really shook me up, I shut off all the negative input. I stopped listening to the news I was hearing from people that I trusted, from acquaintances, and from general media outlets. I stopped listening to the news altogether. While I was online, advertising my outdoor classes, I stopped reading what other people were posting because their words were so fear filled.

I also managed by maintaining my normal practices, such as daily tai chi, meditations, breath work, and being outside. After the initial panic hit me, I went to a local park and did calming breath work to relieve the stress effect. I focused on doing more breath work to calm my mind and keep me thinking clearly. Despite cutting off social media and news, I could still feel the stress vibes coming from all around me, so I consciously worked to keep them at bay.

I also used some of the down time to build my community and business in new ways, using socially distant methods like more outside events and livestreaming to gather together. Being out in nature heals us more than being in a room or building. Being outdoors connects us to our environment, which can help with feelings of disconnection and isolation too.

I think I've navigated the Clickety-Clack by continuing to use the tools I have been using for years. Maintaining the habit of a daily self-care ritual or practice during times of calm makes it super easy to maintain that self-care during times of stress when I need it the most. I've kind of embraced this topsy-turvy COVID situation as an opportunity to view and conduct my business and life in a slightly more connected way. Funny how isolations and quarantine restrictions made me reach out to others more.

I love the yin-and-yang balance of it all!

What tools do you recommend for staying peaceful in a seemingly toxic world?

The number one thing I would recommend is to eliminate what seems toxic. That might mean shutting off the news or changing how we perceive a situation. Changing my thoughts from being negative about COVID to seeing it as an opportunity to grow in new ways was huge.

Don't stay focused solely on the negative news coming in. Be sure to also spend time caring for what you love, like yourself! It is a great tool, to take care of yourself, and if that means shutting off what's toxic, do it. Put on your own oxygen mask first. Don't spend all your time indoors or alone. That's just not healthy. Get outside in nature.

When you're down, stay connected to other people to give yourself a sense of belonging in the world. Meet with people online or outside, even if it's just to stop in the park and talk about the weather.

Have a meaningful self-care daily practice that's not just rote, physical exercise, but actual self-care that's healthy and strengthens your mind as well as body. Not all exercise is healthy; some of it hurts us in the long term by wearing down joints or causing more stress responses in the body. Exercise shouldn't cause stress when we're trying to stay calm. You could practice tai chi, yoga, meditation, dancing— whatever works for you— but make sure you do it every day because you never know what the day is going to throw at you.

The day the quarantine started, I had no idea what was going on. I was working all day. I stopped as I normally did at the grocery store on my way home. I was out of toilet paper, and of course, I couldn't find any. That started the Clickety-Clack for me. One minute you're in the store for TP like normal, then everything's changed and you're begging for tissue from friends. To have daily self-care is paramount for mind, body, and spirit health every day, especially when chaos comes.

About the Author

With over twenty years of daily breath work practice, Lea Williamson is an expert (ShiFu) of qigong breathing. With teaching certifications in various styles of qigong, tai chi, and hands-on healing modalities, Lea's understanding of healthy human movement expresses itself through her inspirational classes. Working with local community classes led her to develop video tutorials on her popular YouTube channel and Facebook outlets for Beachside QiGong and Tai Chi.

At forty, Lea utilized her breath skills to overcome her intense lifelong fear of water by learning to surf. Her experiences with chi arts and surfing alchemized into an Amazon number one New Release book, *Surfing the Sea of Chi*, an empowering personal story combining surfing, chi arts, physics, and the art of being human. Lea's most recent endeavors focus on community building through Surfing Chi socials and workshops, co-founding BAM Community, and speaking with the Smithsonian's *WaterWays* exhibit, exploring the American relationship with water. Her message of personal empowerment through loving self-care resonates to all seeking an inspired, balanced life.

To learn qigong and tai chi tools to help manage your self-health care, visit Lea's website and sign up for the free e-newsletter or become a video member at BeachsideQigong.com.

Ariel Yarger

How has the Clickety-Clack shown up in your life?

The Clickety-Clack comes in different ways. There is a soft, steadier Clickety-Clack that is the normal day-to-day: *I thought we were doing this. Oh my gosh, that did not work. Why did that come up?* Those events are the day-to-day *stop-and-gos* that happen.

Then, there are major Clickety-Clacks. They are like going down a hill where the incline is growing steeper, and things are not clicking into place. The ride may become fast or loud, and you know: *This is a major deal.* You know you need to pay attention to it and do something if you can. Sometimes, you cannot. Sometimes, you must wait until it slows down on its own, giving you time to react and respond.

I experience the everyday things that have to do with raising children, taking care of the house, and homeschooling. Sometimes, things do not go as I want, I do not get a job done like I wanted, or I do not even get to a job. Those kinds of events are minor. Then, there have been a couple of major ones. One was the birth of our child with special needs. We had no idea; he was simply born with Down Syndrome. It was a heavy-duty Clickety-Clack for a few minutes, and then I recognized what was happening, asked my questions, and we went on, taking things as they came.

The second big one was the death of our seventeen-year-old son from a lighting strike. It was very sudden, very hard. We were never expecting that, of course. We were traveling. My husband was gone on a trip; he had left that day. I was heading to Phoenix from Colorado with five of the children in the car. The older children were home working and doing what they normally did because they were older teenagers. I got a call on the road: *Your son has been struck by lightning. He is unconscious and not responding.*

I was on a highway, a six-lane highway, in the middle lane where construction was going on, and traffic was bumper-to-bumper in all lanes. I did not know where the exits were, and I did not know how I was going to turn around. I mentioned that to the police officer on the phone, and he said, "Lady, I am not kidding. This is not a joke."

I thought: *Yeah, I get it. I understand.* I said to him, "I cannot get off the road." He did not understand that I was stuck. So, I merged over, got off the road, turned around, and headed back home. At that moment, I knew we were headed into a place we had never been. In the car, our special needs son was not affected by this at all; he did not know what was going on. One of my sons started looking through the Bible for scripture verses, and one of my sons took my phone and started calling people he knew would pray. The rest of us prayed.

They asked, "Do you think he is still alive?"

Being totally honest, I said, "I do not think so, but we do not know. So, let's just wait until we get there."

We were probably about an hour down the road, and that experience began to develop like all things do. Then it simply was: *Okay, let's get back home. Pick up my stuff, piece by piece.* There we were.

How did you navigate the Clickety-Clack?

The softer Clickety-Clacks happen any day. Sometimes I lose it and ask: *Why?* When I don't hear an answer, I think: *I am not going to know why. So, what is the next thing I need to do?* I then ask myself: *What is the next step I need to do in this moment? What do I need to put aside at this moment because I have something else I need to do?* That is what happens during the softer Clickety-Clacks.

I had systems in place that worked with a large family. These systems would pick up the slack in smaller places. All the older kids had a buddy. We have eleven children, so the older four or five had buddies the longest. They would have a buddy who was a younger child. They kept an eye on their buddy, let me know if there was a problem, and kept track of where they were and what they were doing. There was a general consensus that if we kept things picked up that made everything seem organized and orderly, and it was easier to move through things.

When the harder Clickety-Clacks arrive, the first thing I think is: *It is okay. I am not alone in this. Spirit is breathing me, Spirit is working with me, Spirit already knows all the details of this situation. I just need to calm down enough to be able to pick up some of that.* My special needs son was the first child who looked right into my eyes. I looked right back into those Down Syndrome eyes, and I said, "You are different than the others."

I asked the doctor what she thought, and she replied, "Oh no, he is fine."

Within fifteen minutes of returning to my room, there was a pediatrician explaining about my son. So, we knew. Of all the things that could have happened with this special needs son, Down Syndrome was the best, in a way. Number one: Down Syndrome is a chromosomal abnormality that survives to birth. Number two: he is the picture of love and forgiveness. In a family of thirteen, having one person who is usually loving, happy, and content most of the time is like a soothing balm for the whole family. He did suffer meningitis at fifteen weeks, and he is deaf as a result. He has other mental issues, so he lives as if he is four or five years old and is a happy guy. We took it one day at a time and treated him like a normal baby, a normal child. I put away all developmental milestone timings and let him be who he was.

What tools do you recommend for staying peaceful in a seemingly toxic world?

I did not have all these tools and understandings when I was raising my children. I have come to them in the last several years as my life and responsibilities calmed down, and I had the opportunity to investigate things.

The first thing that has always been with me for as long as I can remember is a scripture verse that says: *He will never leave you nor forsake you.* (Deut. 31:6, NIV) The Power that creates and breathes is with me; I have always known this. That Power notifies me what's going on and tells me what to say. Outside of structured religion and church, it is always there, so I know I am not alone. That knowledge is helpful. Sometimes, I need to remember I am not on my own, that I do not have to do it myself. I need to step back and take a deep breath. I did not always feel or accept that Spirit loves and adores me, but that knowledge has come to me. My coaching instructor introduced me to that concept, and I still yearn for confirmation. I turn to this knowledge for strength.

I invite you to speak these words to yourself in the presence of the Clickety-Clack:

- *Okay, you got this.*
- *You got this because you are loved.*
- *The best is wanted for you.*
- *There is help for what happens.*
- *You are entitled and designed to have the best, so let's go for it.*
- *Let's be ready for the best.*

I am more optimistic than pessimistic, but I have a judgmental side, a critical-to-become-better side, that gets in the way sometimes. I have learned that once I know I am okay, I can drop the judgment about myself, about what I do, about what others do. The biggest part is to realize I can only take care of this minute right now. I cannot do anything about what happened five minutes ago, ten years ago, or forty years ago. I cannot worry about that.

There is no way I know what the future holds. We are all feeling that right now with this pandemic situation. This is unimaginable to me. I have my own opinions about it, but I am not going to share them. I want to stay in this moment, consider what I can or should do in the next moment, what I feel best about.

As a child, as a teenager with peer pressure, as an adult, as a parent—I have kept my emotions under control. When our son died, I spent my release time in the car, when I was driving by myself. It did not happen all the time because I still had a house full of kids. So, whenever I was in the car by myself, I would release the great emotions I might be feeling at that time, so that I could remain strong and capable for the kids.

Now, I concentrate on each emotion, asking: *How does it feel? Is it a good one? Is a bad one?* No matter what the emotion is, I sit with it. Then, I let it pass and let it become less. Then, I deal with whatever it is I need to do next. Basically, *all is well.* Whatever difficult situation is going on *will pass.* My life of over sixty-eight years has proved this true. Nothing remains the same; there is always change.

I have learned more about meditation. I have learned about being quiet with myself; I am still learning that. I have learned how important taking a breath and letting it out is—then maybe taking a couple more. Sometimes when I take a deep breath in and let a deep breath out, I say the word *release* slow on the exhale. That allows me to face what it is I am to face at the moment and decide what to do.

About the Author

I see motherhood as a sacred, vital, intentional calling for women and one of the most challenging and rewarding roles a woman will ever experience. I am the mother of eleven adult children. My deep love and concern for children fires my desire to help and encourage mothers. I am a Certified Transformational Life Coach. I work with mothers through crisis moments, difficult behaviors, surprising life events, and the normal day-to-day challenges. I work with mothers in groups and privately to help them grow and expand as women and mothers. Mothers who work with me will discover they are valuable and capable. They will also acquire tools and strategies to handle any challenges. They will be able to stay calm, be strong, and take care of their child in powerful, graceful, and loving ways.

If you are a mother (or father) struggling with an issue or situation and you would like another mother's point of view or help, you can contact me at arielcoachingmoms@gmail.com. We can also schedule free, twenty-minute strategy call. You can also request a PDF of "10 Household Hacks" I find helpful.

Conclusion

As you reach the end of this book, our hope as the publisher is that you have been inspired by the incredible people we invited to share insights, stories, tips, and tools for navigating the Clickety-Clack of life and staying peaceful within, even when things around you are seemingly toxic.

You may have noticed we used the word *seemingly* in front of the word *toxic*. This is for a specific purpose. Many of our authors love the world and are able to accept whatever is happening around them, still seeing the world as good. Because they use the tools they shared with you, they are either unphased by outward appearances, or in many cases, the time they stay in the negative passes quickly. Seeing the world as toxic is ultimately a choice. One can look at the same event and see it as toxic, or a challenge, a learning experience, or, as some say, "It is what it is." It's all perspective.

As you read our authors' answers to the three questions, did you feel connected to any of them or their perspectives?

If you connected to any of our contributors in strong and meaningful ways, we suggest you reach out to them. Look up the people, websites, programs, or products they mentioned within their chapter of the book.

Our wish for you—like those we invited to be in this book—is to be a walking, talking demonstration of being able to stay neutral, calm, and peaceful no matter what is happening in the outside world.

Thank you for reading this book!

Keith Leon S.

Multiple International Award-Winning Author, Speaker, and Publisher

LeonSmithPublishing.com

BeyondBeliefPublishing.com

About the Publisher

In 2004, Babypie Publishing was founded by entrepreneurs Keith and Maura Leon when they decided to self-publish their co-authored book, *The Seven Steps to Successful Relationships*. When Babypie published its second book, Keith Leon's, *Who Do You Think You Are? Discover the Purpose of Your Life*, a few years later—implementing a large marketing campaign that introduced the book to over a million people on the first day it came out—both books became bestsellers overnight.

After the success of their first two titles, Keith and Maura were approached by another author who believed they could take his book to bestseller status as well. They decided to give it a shot, and Warren Henningsen's book, *If I Can You Can: Insights of an Average Man*, became an international bestseller the day it was released.

Before long, Babypie Publishing was receiving manuscript submissions from all over the world and publishing such titles as Ronny K. Prasad's, *Welcome to Your Life*; Melanie Eatherton's,

The 7-Minute Mirror, and Maribel Jimenez and Keith Leon's, *The Bake Your Book Program: How to Finish Your Book Fast and Serve It Up HOT!*

With a vision to make an even greater impact, Babypie Publishing began offering comprehensive writing and publishing programs, as well as a full range of à-la-carte services to support independent authors and innovative professionals in getting their message out in the most powerful and effective manner. In 2015, Keith and Maura developed the YouSpeakIt book program to make it easy, fast, and affordable for busy entrepreneurs and cutting-edge health practitioners to get their mission and message out to the world.

In 2016, Leon Smith Publishing was created as the new home for Babypie, YouSpeakIt, and future projects. In 2018, Beyond Belief Publishing was added as an imprint for spiritual and esoteric titles.

Whether you're a transformational author looking for writing and publishing services, or a visionary leader ready to take your life and work to the next level, we thank you for visiting our website at LeonSmithPublishing.com, and look forward to serving you.

Made in the USA
Middletown, DE
05 November 2020

23417395R00113